THE HUMMINGBIRD PROJECT

Creating from Scratch

Vickie Frémont

Translated from French by Sophie Schrago

CALEC - TBR Books
New York - Paris

Copyright © 2023 by Vickie Frémont
All rights reserved. No part of this publication may be reproduced, distributed, or transmitted in any form or by any means, without prior written permission.
TBR Books is a program of the Center for the Advancement of Languages, Education, and Communities. We publish researchers and practitioners who seek to engage diverse communities on topics related to education, languages, cultural history, and social initiatives.
CALEC - TBR Books
750 Lexington Avenue, 9th floor
New York, NY 10022
USA
www.calec.org | contact@calec.org
www.tbr-books.org | contact@tbr-books.org
ISBN 978-1-63607-373-6 (Hardback)
ISBN 978-1-63607-375-0 (Paperback)
ISBN 978-1-63607-374-3 (eBook)
Library of Congress Control Number: 2023930978
Translated from *Le projet Colibri : créer à partir de rien* (2022) by Vickie Frémont. Published by TBR Books.

Dedication

This book is for you both, with all my gratitude.

Dear Tracy, thank you for your trust and for the children of Ambohitra

Dear Jean-Jacques, I will never forget the joy and pride that my Tecsup students in Trujillo felt when they learned that the French Ambassador to Peru would come–in person– to see their work exhibited. Heartfelt thanks for this moment.

Vickie Frémont

Preface

I had the pleasure of meeting Vickie Frémont in Peru a few years ago as part of a tour she was doing, with great enthusiasm, within the network of French cultural establishments. I would even call this a communicative enthusiasm because it was not only a question for her of exhibiting the original, colorful, and creative works that she learned to make with recycled materials, fabrics, pieces of wood, paper, buttons, or any other object that comes to mind, provided that in the end it is harmonious and speaks to the imagination...for her, it was a question of involving those who participated in her workshops in unpretentious joy.

Neither simply the business of artmaking nor simply the art of communication, Vickie's idea is having fun, imagining, assembling, and creating. It is based on the journey one takes within oneself and the communion with one's surroundings. By the modesty of the means it uses, and by its philosophy, which draws from certain ancient wisdoms, Vickie's aesthetic practice can remind us of the Amerindian legend of the hummingbird, which we know quite well in some parts of Peru: it is a legend in which this tiny bird valiantly does its part to save the forest from the fire. This legend, and Vickie's work, remind us, on a planet that men's dreams of grandeur have endangered, that we must not neglect any detail, any effort, and above all, that we must think in terms of the best way to go about these efforts, in solidarity with all people of the world.

The marvelous Kenyan Wangari Maathai, recipient of the 2004 Nobel Peace Prize, puts forth this allegory; it is not surprising that today another girl from Africa, an artist and a wonderful citizen of the world, Vickie Frémont, takes up the legend of the hummingbird to make it the emblem of a project and the title of a book.

Because to speak, in a somewhat technocratic way, of the imperative need to promote the circular economy, remains much too far below the philosophical and aesthetic dimension of the project. It's ultimately a story of all our essential humanity.

Only Vickie Frémont, with her personal experience and aesthetic research, was as qualified from either a logical or symbolic point of view to carry out and represent the work of such a project.

We can only thank her and wish her and her project all the success they deserve.

Jean Jacques Beaussou, former French Ambassador to Peru (2011- 2014).

Table of Contents

Dedication 1
Preface 3
Introduction 7
Let's Revisit My Workshops 17
   I – Upright Men's Workshop 17
   II – Me to Myself 28
   III – The Day I Decided to Be Beautiful... 40
   IV – Masks Workshop 46
   V – Men's Workshop - Kitchen Staff 54
   VI – Professional Development Workshop 60
   VII – A Joyful Learning Process 76
Beginning of the Pandemic 83
Official Start of the Pandemic 98
The Hummingbird Project in Times of Covid-19 112
A Hummingbird Project in Ambohitra - Madagascar 116
Another Hummingbird Project...Mancey 126
Description of Some of the Videos that we Propose 133
   1 - Creating "people" from hangers 133
   II – "Knitting plastic bag yarn" 138
   III – "My Secret Bag" 142
   IV - Cutting and Gluing 144
For Mia 148
Our Readings during the Pandemic 152
Table of Illustrations 166
Acknowledgments 169
Notes 171
Post Scriptum 173
About TBR Books 174
About CALEC 176

Introduction

My book invites you to experience some of the workshops of the Hummingbird Project that have been offered to all – adults and children alike – in New York, where I currently live, but also in places I have traveled during my various trips abroad.

Wherever I have stopped, wherever I stop, my workshops are a meditation centered around the following mantra:

"What do you see?"

Silence.

This silence allows you to "see" better within you and around you.

Our hands are our tools; they create.

Workshop time is a time of tranquility and peace.

"The tremors of the earth unite us because we all come from the same poem"

The Hummingbird Project is my personal and powerful vision of Africa: to create from "nothing", an art that many still consider without much interest, or intellectualize by bringing it into the very chic field of contemporary art, or even place in the realm of an art that some refer to with a certain militant activism to preserve the environment.

The Hummingbird Project is quite simply a journey within oneself and a source of infinite discoveries.

"Every night, her dad or mom would call her for a session of 'what did you see?'. There seemed to be no end to what she was seeing, and yet her dad hadn't told her much, but kept asking questions so that she would find the answers within herself..." **(1)**

The question: "What do you see?" finds a multitude of answers in all these things that can be recycled. It opens a wide field of possibilities.

The Hummingbird Project was inspired by the Native American legend of the hummingbird, the same legend that moved Wangari Maathai, the first African woman to receive the Nobel Peace Prize. Wangari Maathai had started the Green Belt movement that replanted millions of trees in an effort to halt desertification in Kenya.

I ask us, today, to identify with this tiny bird fighting a huge forest fire that the other animals watch fly from the river to the forest with a drop of water in its little beak.

To the animals that taunt him, he simply replies..."I'm doing my best." Any resemblance to similar situations is, of course, not coincidental! We need to do our best in all circumstances, with our hands as our only tools.

The ambition of the Hummingbird Project is to create from "nothing", including from the objects which we get rid of because they "are no longer useful." So wouldn't "doing one's best" be offering us a break, during which our hands return to their primary role – to create – to come out of ourselves, from our inner prison, to be the creators of our daily life?

My workshops put adults and children on the same level, with common ground: having fun, relaxing, and calming anxieties that sometimes overwhelm us in the face of events or a situation we cannot control, wearing us down and preventing us from moving forward.

To feed our imagination and stimulate our creativity, nothing could be more intriguing than little plastic bottles, pieces of fabric cut from used clothes, plastic bags that we continue to find in large quantities, boxes, gems of junk, old newspapers, magazine pages! And sometimes, hangers are picked up in the dustbins of dry cleaners and transformed into people who represent those from Africa, Europe, Asia, or elsewhere.

I undertake each workshop as a journey in which I lead the sometimes skeptical participants, children or adults. The key word: freedom!

Whether online, in class, or in community spaces, our voice is replaced by music, or sometimes even by complete silence because it is meant to be an inner journey for the participants. My teaching can be summed up with the idea of being present to help push open the doors to one's inner self.

Case in point; these hangers. What a source of inspiration! Here is the story of the Traveling Penguin workshop in a nutshell:

A few years ago, I did three afternoons of workshops with a group of students from an engineering school in Trujillo, Peru: I gave each student 4 hangers and two instructions:

- Look at these hangers and translate what you see into objects. Create three objects.

- The fourth hanger can be included in any of these three projects.

For these future engineers, the first challenge was to forget all the technical tools they were used to using. At their disposal, they had only a pair of scissors, a little white glue, and their two hands.

They looked at the recycled materials on the table: pieces of fabric, old magazines, pieces of wool of different colors, some beads, some sheets of silk paper, scissors and glue, and a personal, different, additional gift for each student: two large pieces of African fabric.

These brilliant students, future elites of their country, seemed very dubious, a bit annoyed. "How can we, in the 21st century, do without all the technology we have to move forward better and faster?" A student would later admit: "I liked it, creating just with my two hands. It was an extraordinary experience!"

Antonio, one of the students seated at a secluded table, was doing and redoing. He had surrounded himself with a thousand objects. Very calmly, he was grabbing materials and adjusting them to each other. He was completely focused, locked in his bubble, barely moving.

During the afternoon, he made a spectacular bird, a very realistic little dog, and also a purple penguin that he gave me and which made him laugh a lot: "I used two hangers for this one. He's a Traveling Penguin like you!"

The dean of the establishment, during a visit to the hall, was so impressed by the students' achievements that he decided that the school would keep most of their works for a permanent exhibition.

The Hummingbird Project is a series of timeless workshops that reveal to us the obvious truth: that our hands are our most precious tools. Everything that is invented is born from our hands.

My workshops take a snapshot of important moments in our daily lives. They are like a meditation, a reflection where we don't explain the why or the how or analyze historical events; books and history teachers have their role to play which I do not seek to replace.

Rather, the workshops simply invite us to open ourselves to the world and in turn to open up to our inner selves. This opening, wherein our hands are our tools and the work they do during the time of the workshop, allows the rushing mind to settle down and the body to rest as much as possible, by slowing down the sometimes frantic pace that both mind and body are constantly exposed to in today's world. The Hummingbird Project workshops bring us back to ourselves, so that we can find the resources necessary to love who we are through our creations. Our workshops also bring joy to all the various learning processes. Those are concrete tools with which teachers, if they wish, can find ways to communicate with their students and colleagues.

I'm going to tell you about some of my workshops. I do not use a pre-scripted method: for each workshop, I prepare myself for an encounter, ready to offer as much as I receive. And each of these encounters contributes to personal growth, both for the participants and for myself.

The Traveling Penguin

Travel the world.
You will learn about
its issues.

Ewondo proverb Cameroon

Let's Revisit my Workshops

I - Upright Men's Workshop

25th Commemoration of the Tutsi genocide in Rwanda. The workshop takes place in New York with students from a private high school and involves the creation of large puppet dolls. The "Upright Men" workshop was inspired by Small Country, the novel by French-Rwandan writer Gaël Faye, better known by our students as a rapper.

On the eve of the Tutsi genocide in Rwanda in 1994, young Gaby, the hero of Small Country, lives with his family in Burundi, a country bordering Rwanda where the same peoples, Tutsis and Hutus, live together. In parallel, I also revisited the work of British visual artist Bruce Clarke: "Abantu Bahagaze Bemye" in Kinyarwanda or "Les Hommes Debout" in French.

Following an order from the National Commission for the Fight against the Genocide of Rwanda, he painted larger than life figures of men, women and children – portraits of 7 to 10 meters high – silent images of anonymous but familiar characters that are symbols of the dignity of human beings confronted with the dehumanization that genocide entails. These paintings were hung on the facades of the sites of massacres in Rwanda but also in symbolic places of memory and history in Europe and Africa. By their presence, these hangings are, and continue to be, the link between the community of the living and the victims of the genocide and symbolize the universality of the fight for life.

The challenge proposed to our students was to create characters of a size of 50 to 90 cm in height from hangers shaped into human form of 33 cm in height.

In *Small Country*, Gaby asks the following questions:

- "The war between the Tutsis and Hutus," Gaby asks his father, "is it because they don't have the same land?"
- "No," his father responds, "they have the same country."
- "So...they don't have the same language."
- "No, they speak the same language."
- "So, they don't have the same God?"
- "No, they have the same God."
- "So...Why are they at war?"
- "Because they don't have the same nose."

And that was the end of the discussion. It was all very odd. I'm not sure Papa really understood it, either".

Gaël Faye, *Small Country*.

We spent ten minutes together, recalling the historical context of the Rwandan genocide: on the evening of April 6, 1994, the plane of Juvénal Habyarimana – Rwanda's Hutu president – was shot down. The genocide of the Tutsis then began on April 7, 1994. In less than a hundred days, nearly a million men, women and children were killed amidst the general indifference of the international community.

The students took turns reading or reciting one of Gaby's questions as well as the answer given by his father. To read these words, as simple as they are absurd, was a prerequisite for starting to work.

By creating these great characters with their hands, I offered the students a work of remembrance. Gaël Faye's book stood not too far away, nor were the photos of Bruce Clarke's large paintings. Before starting the workshop, we also listened to two texts rapped by Gaël Faye.[1]

Only two students had read *Small Country*. I learned later that the teachers, finding Gaël Faye's novel too violent and emotionally difficult to bear for their young students, did not want them to read it. I pointed out to them that *Small Country* won the Goncourt Prize Youth Jury in France in 2016.

Together with the students, we established the link between our workshop, the content of the book, and the work of Bruce Clarke – "The Upright Men". In 1994, none of them had been born. Nevertheless, they shared with me the difficulty they sometimes face when it comes to learning what is happening in African countries. Even though they are all

---

[1] https://www.youtube.com/watch?v=XTF2pwr8lYk
https://www.youtube.com/watch?v=Au5k7NzUkIk

active on social media, they rarely research topics concerning Africa. When it comes to Africa, internet discourse is often related to music, sports, or natural disasters. Therefore, they only vaguely know that this genocide took place: one more atrocity that occurred in Africa, this continent that they were told is poor and still savage.

Several sets of material were missing. The teachers who opened the workshop to students from three classes could not tell me the final number of participants as they hadn't received the confirmation of who would attend or not: so instead of the 18 students expected, 25 showed up to participate in the workshop.

It was out of the question not to welcome them all. I usually always carry extra material with me, just in case...I had 3 additional sets available, including my demo kit that I needed to keep. I then consulted the students: very few of them knew how to sew, and even if the sewing work did not require great skills, some students found it more productive to work in pairs. It seemed to me to be an interesting and innovative idea.

Then I explained to them what they had to do and how they could use the equipment available to them in large bags.

Equipment:

- a hanger already shaped in human form with a head, arms, body and legs
- a small ball of wool to be wrapped around the head to form the face, leaving some space to tie the hair
- forty pre-cut wool threads (approximately 30 cm) for the hair
- a pair of scissors
- sewing needles
- three small spools of thread (black, white and brown)
- 50 cm of lining foam
- two pieces of one yard of different African fabrics

- two DVDs with about twenty pieces of pre-cut fabrics of 1 cm/50 cm
- a small brush for the glue provided by the school
- a small plastic pouch with glass beads and jewelry wire. Everything is provided in sufficient quantity.

I was amused by the way they engaged with the project. I had advised the pairs to divide up the tasks, but to no avail: they did everything together!

Even the task of rolling the wool to create the head and face was done with four hands: a real achievement! Then they tied the pieces of wool to make the hair, still with four hands – fascinating!

We had installed two of our "Upright Men" on the board so that the students could assess the size and the accessorizing, but also to prove to them that it was possible to create large dolls from the shaped hangers we provided them, since some students seemed to doubt it and were considering drastically cutting into the large pieces of fabric provided.

It was also the occasion to offer a quick introduction to the basics of sewing so that they could put together the clothes of their dolls.

Remarks:

"We found a way not to sew!" proudly claimed two students.

"Great! But no staples or glue please. You can use pins in a pinch, but they must be safety pins if you have some."

Nevertheless, the students had the freedom to find their own solutions as long as they did not bring in tools. They had sewing needles, scissors and liquid glue available to them for certain accessories but as we told them again: no glue to adjust the clothes. After about fifteen minutes, little faces started to emerge with long hair of different colors depending on the yarns distributed or the locks of false hair offered.

Smiles of amusement appeared on the faces of the students. This also made me smile because, despite them being 14 or 16 years-old, the sight of this transformation generates the same amused astonishment in young and old alike. I almost expected to see the students start playing with their transformed tall dolls!

Covering the small form with thick canvas and foam to reshape and enlarge the doll was a showdown requiring their full attention. The room went silent for about twenty minutes with only the music of Ballaké Sissoko's kora and Vincent Segal's cello in the background. Then came the time to adjust and sew the clothes – long skirts or trousers, each student and each pair having made their choice. For the pairs, this creativity in tandem – in addition to the fact that it enriched the work – also showed its limits. It was at the level of transmission and sharing where everyone did their part generously, it seems.

The students then took the time to shape the hairstyles while their teachers and other instructors came to help, worked on pendants with DVDs for those who wished or helped them finish the seams of the clothes or simply thread needles to allow them to move faster. It was a real joyful collective work, as much for the teachers as for the students!

We had very beautiful and very tall "Upright Men & Women." Two students who had not finished on time during the 2-hour workshop remained in the room. All smiles, they told me how happy the workshop had made them. At first, they were worried and a little uncomfortable because they had read Gaël Faye's book and found the descriptions of certain scenes of violence difficult to imagine. Both were from Jewish families and grew up with the memory of the Holocaust – for them the most terrible of genocides if they had to put them on a scale. So, it was impossible for them to imagine and accept this genocide: more than 800,000 Rwandan Tutsi were massacred within hundred days – those numbers were unimaginable. They therefore felt shaken at the beginning of the workshop.

"And now?"

One of the two recited the following while staring at her work:

"So why did they go to war? Because they don't have the same nose. The discussion ended there. It was all very odd."

"It was all very odd," commented the other student.

A few months later, while going through the photos taken during the workshop, I understood why the students, their French teachers, and those who had come to help described my workshop as a "Therapy Workshop."

Certainly, we have all invested a lot. Certainly, the subject had challenged the students a bit and many were upset that such genocide could still happen at the beginning of the 21st century. However, as students from a prestigious school which was preparing them to enter equally prestigious universities, they seized the opportunity to slow down.

They took advantage of the opportunity offered to them to let their hands go, to create, without worrying about any evaluation. It is sometimes difficult to measure the degree of satisfaction of these teenagers, but obviously something very strong had happened. It hadn't been a miracle, nor a fluke. These young students focused on the creation of "Upright Men" had simply, by becoming creators, paid a beautiful tribute to the memory of the millions forgotten from the Rwandan genocide and all genocides.

The best therapy is simply to create something with your hands, to appreciate the moment of creation, to be present to yourself and to others.

II – ME for MYSELF

The ME for MYSELF workshop took place during a weekend retreat with a group of women in upstate New York.

During this retreat, I accompanied a group of eight women supported by an organization for the rehabilitation and assistance of battered and abused women. The retreat took place in the countryside. The organizers had planned a series of activities, including one of my workshops. I had proposed and set up a two-hour workshop: ME for MYSELF.

I met the group in midtown Manhattan at 7 a.m. on a Saturday morning. We all got onto a minibus. The group consisted of a chef, a psychotherapist, and a social worker coordinator who drove the minibus and eight women aged between 30 and 60.

We arrived late in the morning at a large manor in a beautiful, hidden and peaceful place in the woods.

The first task was to make sure that we were not miss anything of for different meals to be prepared during the weekend.

For lunch, we ate vegetable sandwiches. The chef warned us that she had planned only vegetarian meals, as most of the women were vegetarian.

*I almost asked for help, but my voice was inaudible, that's weird, isn't it?
And then if I had asked for help, it wouldn't have made sense to me anymore.*

P.

Groups formed spontaneously, one to help the chef peel vegetables, another to put the bags in the rooms and air them. The joyful and good-natured chef enlivened the conversations from the kitchen, conversations that she punctuated with great bursts of laughter.

Although the atmosphere was relaxed, the women maintained a certain distance from what I would call the "management." Half of these women already knew each other, and the other half had just met. Despite the customary use of first names, all continued to call me "Madame."

The important thing was that there was a good atmosphere of already developing camaraderie. These women were all going through the similar experiences of suffering, but the fact that they participated in this retreat was for them an opportunity to let go and to take some distance away from their heavy everyday life.

After lunch, while some were resting, reading, or sleeping, I took a walk in the countryside with M. and T., who explained to me that they expected a lot from this retreat without really being able to put their expectations into words. They asked questions about the ME for MYSELF workshop but did not insist on knowing more. I felt them to be a little tense and disillusioned.

They had been participating in this retreat for 3 years and this was the first time that an art and recycling workshop had been offered. Of course, they trusted the organizers, but they were not convinced of the usefulness of all the activities offered. However, they were curious: "So, we'll see!" they concluded.

I better understood their reluctance as I participated in the middle of the afternoon in the writing workshop led by M. the therapist. This workshop was also new to the program. Anything out of their routine seemed to cause them stress, and the thought of even writing a line on any subject felt impossible. M. had to speak to each person individually to reassure them before starting the workshop. After dinner, we cleaned and did the dishes.

We finally started the ME for MYSELF workshop later that evening. It was expected that each participant would sit anywhere they wanted, the manor being big enough to give them this freedom as long as they chose a well-lit and easily accessible place. In the meantime, I presented the workshop, distributed the material, and answered questions.

Each participant received a large paper bag that we opened together. I explained how the workshop was going to unfold, saying that a certain discipline was necessary for the project to go as smoothly as possible and so that they could give themselves over to their creativity.

I took the materials out of the bag, one item at the time:
- 1 hanger shaped into a person which would be the base of the doll they would create.
- a small ball of wool for the head: I took the time to show them how to unroll the wool to shape the face and arrange the hair.
- 40 pre-cut threads of wool (about 30 cm long) to be used for the hair. I also gave them the choice of strands of false hair that could be attached to the head.
- a pair of scissors, which would quickly prove useful
- sewing needles, to which they were free to help themselves, including the very large needle needed to place the locks of false hair
- black sewing thread
- 4 pieces of fabric (approximately 50 cm x 50 cm) for the clothes
- 4 to 5 pieces of fabric of different sizes and colors to accessorize if deemed necessary.
- A small plastic pouch with glass beads, elastic thread and 7 cowries (small shells)

Finally, I explained to them how to place the clothes (skirts, tunics or pants), and answered questions. They listened attentively; none seemed anxious. On the contrary, they were smiling and visibly relaxed. They asked questions about the use of cowries.

I replied that it is very much a part of African traditions. In Africa as in China, a long time ago, cowries were a barter currency. Today, while it is a small lucky charm for some, and an object of worship among the Yorubas in Nigeria, for some in Japan it is an ancient custom to hold cowries in the hand during childbirth.

Cowries can be included in a necklace; they can be added to hair or sewn to clothing. There were seven in the bag, intentionally because the number 7 is important in the Cosmos. It is a spiritual number that corresponds to knowledge, analysis, and luck. It is a belief that I shared with them and that they could deepen later if they wished.

I distributed additional pieces of fabric, which they were free to cut and add them to those they already had. They were not required to use the cowries: they could leave them in the bag that they would place at the end of their table for another participant who would like to collect them...

- "And what about some music?" they asked.
- "There will be no music. Sit where it suits you best. Silence will really help you to create."

From ME for MYSELF is a silent meditation.

Once they confirmed to me that they understood the process, I let them work at their own pace.

"Only my hands speak with me, they help me enter into myself and connect with my heart, regulate my breathing. If there is a challenge, it must not scare me, because its purpose is to lead to a meeting with a woman or a man who looks like me and whom I see as very beautiful or very handsome, my twin sister or my twin brother."

Although the table in the hall was very large and could accommodate them all, several women moved around, two asked to go to their rooms, one went to the kitchen, another settled on a small table near the fireplace. The coordinator took care of the lighting before sitting in turn at the large table near the chef and M. the therapist. They all took part in the workshop.

When I began to move from one participant to the other, I noticed that, very quickly, they were concentrating, had few questions, and visibly had the desire to be left alone. When the workshop was finally over, late in the evening, we gathered around the large table in the main hall.

There was excitement in the air, old smiles that seemed to resurface from childhood, and an eagerness to recount the experience.. I suggested that each woman, one after the other, talk about their experience and present their twin by naming them...

It was a long and beautiful evening, very lively and warm, sharing experiences of creation.

"I experienced this workshop like a birth, alone and with bare hands.

I thought of these indigenous women whose names I no longer remember who go alone to give birth in the forest. At first, I thought that I couldn't do it; I'm not used to doing that. I would have liked to have a model, but in the end, it would have been useless. I panicked, especially when making the head and placing the hair. I almost asked for help, but my voice was inaudible; that's weird, isn't it? And then if I had asked for help, it wouldn't have made sense to me anymore."

P. the dean laughed as she introduced us to her twin, which she had finally finished, with apprehension but also joy in having managed to create it alone.

S. started the gospel "Take me to the water" sung by all of us to celebrate her twin:

"It made me feel good, I'm so happy."

"I haven't felt this good in a long time" L. admitted shyly when presenting her twin.

"I am the shadow; Eva is the light. She flies everywhere around me" she confided to us in a whisper. Eva, her twin, wore very sophisticated clothes that contrasted with her very simple and neutral outfit.

X. told us about a Yoruba tradition in Nigeria: The Ibeji statuettes represent twins, considered to be endowed with supernatural powers, beneficial for their family.

If one of the twins dies, it is essential to make a statuette representing the deceased to protect his relatives from the harmful consequences that could cause the separation of his soul from that of his living twin. The Ibeji figurine is therefore the repository of the soul of the dead twin, and it is given the same care as the living one.

When both twins die, it is necessary to make two statuettes so that their spirit can bring benefits and prosperity to their family.

"The Ibeji are always represented by adults. I lost my twin sister when I was 4 years old. I feel like I brought her back to life today, and that completes me."

They gazed at their creations with amazed faces and knowing smiles!

I don't run away, I fly.
Understand, I fly.
Smoke-free, alcohol-free.
I fly, I fly...

M. Sardou

III - "The day I decided to be beautiful...I stopped having the nightmare that has wrecked my nights for many years..."

"The day I decided to be beautiful...I stopped having nightmares..."

I was with a group of teenage girls, 14-16 years old, with whom I had been meeting once a week for several months. They had decided that they were not interested in the project: creating "fashion bags" from plastic baskets (those used to package berries). They had to weave in and tie as many pre-cut pieces of fabric as possible and keep repeating the same pattern. They said that was boring. Faced with their determination, I could have argued that they should not refuse a workshop prepared specifically for them (a discussion that I often had with them). I chose another approach and offered them the "game of history":

"One, two or three of you, depending on the time we have to spend together, will tell us a story about something great that happened to them. While listening, and without commenting, you will work on your little bags. You'll see, it'll be cool. So, the only rule is you must not interrupt the story or stop your work. Who wants to start?"

Surprised for a moment, they hesitated. Finally, M. got up:

"My story is called: 'Why I decided that I am beautiful'"

She was met with shouts of encouragement from her friends: "YEAH!"

"One day I decided that I was beautiful, and I'll tell you why: I was tired of being called ugly and fat at school, but also by my cousins and sometimes by my own mother.

Every night since I was 10, I have had the same nightmare: a shadow visits me, it flies above me, then it falls on me, and I can't do anything or catch it because it's a shadow. I try to push it; I know it's there. I feel it, but it's a shadow. I can't get it out, I'm terrified. I try to scream but no sound comes out of my mouth. The shadow eventually rises in the air again and disappears. I tremble and dare not move. Sometimes I feel like I'm falling into a bottomless pit, I'm falling, I'm falling... It takes me hours to rise to the surface. When I emerge, I am exhausted, dead tired! One day I thought I heard the shadow say that I was ugly, but that's impossible, shadows do not speak... Another time, I thought again that the shadow was talking to me and saying, 'Look at yourself in a mirror you'll see, you're really ugly.' It was crazy!!"

It had been so long since I had been convinced of my ugliness that I hardly ever looked at myself in the mirror. The shadow came back every night, and then one day I looked at myself in a mirror... This was not very long ago..."

As if to make sure they were on board, M. took a moment to look at her friends, sitting at a large circle of tables.

".. Can I continue my story?" "... Sure!"

I found them all to be very attentive, listening, putting on and tying their pieces of fabric.

"Why ugly? What does it mean to be ugly? Who decides who is ugly or not? Ugly, compared to what? To whom?" said M. "Now, I decided to be beautiful: my hair is very thick and frizzy, and I have always let it grow without taking care of it. I brushed and combed it very hard even though it hurt me, and I was able put it into two big braids..."

M.'s voice is muffled and deep at the same time. She speaks very calmly.

"...I looked at my face for a long time, I have no more pimples, and my skin is smooth. As for my nose, yes, it is flat, but I think it goes well with my big eyes. Not 'big' eyes like my cousin Rita would have said, but big eyes, with long eyelashes. And I don't need to tweeze my eyebrows...»

I observed the hands of her friends who were busy working on their little bags.

"...If my eyes had been big, they might have allowed me to make out who that shadow was in my nightmares, but no, my eyes aren't big enough, they're just like two big, pretty almonds; they are a very dark brown, almost black. My mouth matches my nose. I say that because my lips are plump, I like them a lot especially since I read in a magazine that there are stars who perform operations to enlarge their lips and have eager lips... eager to eat life... Yes, I'm going to eat life! Today I'm beautiful, I see the face that the mirror sends back to me. I'm not afraid to look at my face anymore. Yeah, those two big braids look really good on me and make my head pretty."

She smiled as she continued her story."I'm tall, too tall for my age," says my mother. I'm 15 now, but it's true that since the age of 10, I've always been the tallest in the class. I had small breasts; they are still small. I think that one day the shadow said something about my breasts: that they were round like peaches. That's stupid, isn't it? Yes, stupid!!! This nightmare terrorized me, coming back to the surface exhausted me so much that when I woke up, I couldn't remember anything. I was sweating so much that I was soaked! Now that I'm beautiful, I can look at myself, and my mirror shows me a normal body, long legs, neither fat nor thin, just normal! Who dared to say that I was too ugly? My body is like my nose, like my lips; it is strong, it is alive. I look at it and today I know I'm beautiful! Now I'm going to keep looking at my body.

How did I not see how beautiful and strong it is? You know what?! Now that I'm beautiful to myself, I don't have this horrible nightmare anymore, and the shadow is gone... I think the shadow has evaporated..."

She stopped and observed her friends who weren't looking at her, all busy on their basket now, eager to attach all the pieces. Two friends are in tears. Nobody says anything... M. concludes with a big smile: "Girls, today I'm beautiful and that's really important! Enough already! No more nightmares..."

'M. You are beautiful and your story is AMAZING!!!" said S., her best friend, who got up and hugged her.

None of the others wished to speak during the forty minutes that remained. They were busy working on their "fashion bag" and did not make any comment when I put on the music of Manish Vyas (Water Down the Ganges) which they told me another day that they loved. M. has also went to finish her bag. She seemed serene...

Whoever has not yet suffered misfortune does not speak.

Rwandan proverb

IV – MASKS WORKSHOP

As part of workshops offered by a company to its staff.

It may sound a bit silly, but after organizing the "traders' workshop" in New York and the "kitchen brigade workshop" in a very chic restaurant in Cusco, Peru, being able to organize a workshop for a group of men, or women, or transgender people so that they can recoup energy just among themselves seemed perfect. The Hummingbird Project is a moment of meditative relaxation for everyone, and if certain work environments bring together individuals of the same gender, why not? I could adapt.

I tackled the subject with the Peruvian "super machos" I met in Cusco. They agreed that it was fun and friendly. Having a manual activity just among men allowed them to relax completely: in any case, they did not have to be in an almost automatic game of seduction as they would be in the presence of women.

In New York, I was asked at the last minute to offer a relaxation workshop for a group of executives (in the Financial District) who were caught up in a situation of great stress following an enormous workload during a period of intense activity. I accepted the request with a bit of apprehension and a little worry because I hadn't really had time to find out about the participants of the workshop. The only information I received when I was approached about my workshop had been that they were "financial executives in crisis", which did not mean much to me. I usually carry out workshops wherever I'm invited in the world, with women in distress, street children, schoolchildren of all levels but never "Financial District moguls". This was a first. The location of the workshop and the number of participants were provided to me by text message the day before, late in the evening. The Hummingbird Project: "To be used for emergency situations." Why not?

Choice of project: a mask to be decorated with small pieces of fabric in different shapes, patterns and colors. It must be done at a slow pace: choose a fabric, put glue on the mask, and then glue by intertwining the pieces with each other. "Slowing down, picking up pieces": a whole program!

In a hurry, I had to organize the workshop with whatever material I had at my disposal: papier-mâché made masks ready to be decorated, a variety of African fabrics to be cut; a large quantity of recently recycled DVDs, and plastic lacing in several colors. I also brought some literature with several photos of Bamileke elephant masks from Cameroon.

The number of participants was between 15 and 20 maximum. This meant preparations and materials for up to 22-23 people.

And so here I was on an October afternoon on the 20th floor of a New York building, in a large room, naturally lit by large bay windows which filtered in a beautiful autumn light. Long tables placed in a square allowed me to move around easily, and there were comfortable chairs for the participants.

I was asked to arrive half an hour before the start of the workshop. I was accompanied by P., a young intern who was very excited about this new adventure.

I set up the materials and spoke with the Communications Manager, the person who had selected my project after being immediately intrigued by my approach - an approach that she found simple and effective and in which she also wanted to participate.

The gentlemen were very punctual. They were pretty much all in their forties. They quickly glanced at the materials placed on the tables and without preamble, they challenged me:

"So, how are we going to recycle?" It seemed to amuse them. They all had a badge with their first name written on it but nevertheless wanted to introduce themselves one after the other. John, Peter, Henry and the others. Like in a game.

A telephone rang, leading to a short moment of tension. It was a violation of a rule that I set in my workshops and that I never fail to bring up when anybody approaches me for a workshop: no phones (nor leaving to make or receive a call for the whole duration of the workshop).

The one whose phone rang stepped out to answer. He explained to me upon his return that he was expecting this important call. The Communications Manager then calmly addressed the men, explaining she would be notified in the event of an emergency, and that if anyone needed to be contacted, she would, of course, notify them immediately. Then she invited them all to relax:

"Turn off your cell phones. Relax and enjoy!" I could hear whispers from the group who seemingly appreciated this intervention. This may have alleviated their frustration at having to live without their main life/work tool for a few hours. I also appreciated that they agreed to "play the game", so that this workshop time could turn into a simple, complete, and beautiful experience for each of them. However, I kept the possibility of talking about the phone incident again at the end of the workshop open if they wished.

The smile of the Communications Manager and the playful good mood of "P", our intern, who asked them about their work, very quickly helped create a relaxing atmosphere. I started to explain to them what they would have to do, and the conditions under which the workshop would take place, with the possibility for everyone to introduce themselves again at the end by sharing their experience of creating the mask.

"You have an hour and a half to decorate your mask and use the CDs to add ears, taking inspiration from by the Elephant masks of the Bamileke tribe of Cameroon. Forget your watches, let the time flow.

Put each piece of fabric on your mask without leaving any empty space by overlapping the pieces. Choose your pieces before putting glue on the mask; glue and repeat as many times as necessary. Do not cover the eyes."

The last notes of the Oud by Anouar Brahme floated in the air and then the silence of the participants took over. It felt as if we were in a very special place outside of New York where gentlemen in ties lean over papier-mâché masks and glue together small pieces of colored fabric with a brush. This image was a step outside of reality – as if it were from another world, far from the "business is business" motto of New York City, far from the Wall Street bubble where every minute represents sums of money gained or lost.

I accompanied the gentlemen who were no longer part of this reality. They evolved at this precise moment into the Hummingbird Project dimension in which they were asking how to create ears out of DVDs and pre-cut pieces of fabric. Senior executives laughed, played and challenged each other by placing the masks on their faces once they were done.

"Look at me. Look at what I've done." "I'm going to give mine to my daughter."

"We're all done, how do you know exactly how long it takes us to decorate this mask?"

Unanswered question. I adapt my workshops to the time allocated to me. I'm not about performance or a race; without wanting it our hands coach us, and we then become the masters of our own time. I asked them: "What is most important; to finish your mask with an eye on the clock or to appreciate the work you have done? Perhaps both?" I answered, "So don't worry, everything happened exactly at the pace of your meditation." I continued: "The important thing is to make sure that the workshop takes place in such a way as to allow everyone to let go, to breathe, to meditate, and since there are several of you working on the same project, you're also given time to share and exchange. There is no competition. And now, if you wish, the floor is yours."

I noted several of their remarks; all, for the most part, revolved around the fact that they were not artists, that they would never have imagined that they would do what they did "as kids" as part of their job. In their lifestyle, that kind of activity seemed superfluous. Rather, they would share a drink or two at happy hour at the end of the day with colleagues, collapse on the sofa once at home, then wake up very early to start a day of racing against numbers: all this would make part of their daily life, six days a week, and complaining about it is out of the question.

"And you?" asks H. "Did you have any requirements for us and our work?"

"'Requirements' is not the word. Certainly, I want you to respect the time previously agreed upon, and as you may have noticed, I want to make sure that your mobile phone is switched off. I'm not here to evaluate what you are doing. I want to intervene as little as possible in the creative process. From the moment you start the workshop, I simply ensure that the encounter goes well." "The encounter?"

"The encounter with yourself, with the creator that you are!" Smiles appeared on their faces.

"Two hours without a phone, without texting, without a screen, without being on alert and without worrying about it, that is a miracle for me," remarked L.

They all nodded in agreement.

I would have liked to take a picture of these relaxed, almost childish faces. I told them so and it made them laugh a lot...

"Please don't tell our wives what we just did, they think we're traders!!!"

J. 40 years old: "I browse the financial pages of the magazines I receive or subscribe to online. When I was younger, I used to love adventure novels and comic books. I can't remember how long it has been since I last read anything other than these financial pages! Actually, I don't have time to read anything else, it's impossible! I jog every day, fortunately...So, imagine spending an hour pasting pieces of fabrics on a mask and having it make me feel good - it seems like madness!"

The Communications Manager explained to me that this kind of workshop is usually difficult or even impossible to set up. Of course, they have several seminars throughout the year offered by the company's council, but the tight and fluctuating schedule of some executives makes it difficult to organize anything and, in any case, they always have to give priority to training seminars or business trips.

She couldn't believe they could make the workshop happen - because although the Hummingbird Project workshop was not required, it had awoken a lot of curiosity.

I thanked them all for their participation. And these 15 gentlemen in white shirts and ties stood up as one and applauded.

What an improbable Hummingbird Project meeting - a first!

Here are the materials we gave to each of them:

- A pre-formed papier-mâché mask
- A brush and one small paper cup for liquid glue
- A pair of scissors
- Pre-cut pieces of fabric
- 4 CDs
- About 20 pieces of fabric (ranging in size from 1cm to 50 cm)
- 50cm of plastic lacing

Masks are the means of transmitting something beyond us

Amadou Hampâté Ba

V – MEN'S WORKSHOP - Kitchen Staff

Although the request was made to me two days before the actual date of the workshop, things seemed less complicated to set up in Cusco than they were in New York. I undoubtedly had less apprehension, and I better understood the work of the kitchen staff.

As part of a general tour with the Alliances Française in Peru, I spent a week in Cusco, a magnificent city in the Peruvian Andes. Two days before my return to Lima, I was invited to give a workshop for the kitchen staff of the hotel where I was staying. They were rather friendly, which immediately piqued my curiosity, and I accepted them with much enthusiasm.

The hotel manager wanted to offer one of my workshops to the hotel cooks who had worked hard all of July and still had much of the tourist season ahead of them...The hotel was superb and had a very large restaurant that was full every night.

I devoted two evenings to preparing small dolls with the few soft hangers and accessories that were left from my previous workshops on different sites. I also had a day of walking coming up, during which I was planning on finding and buying Andean fabrics.

This workshop also took me out of my comfort zone because of the participants' circumstances and demographics. In either case, whether it was the "financial" workshop or this one, the participants were exposed to an intense professional rhythm. The kitchen staff worked non-stop every day. In this very touristy city, the hotel and its restaurant were not only very popular but had a gastronomic reputation to protect against the competition. The management had set us up in a lounge overlooking the hotel, which made me smile and think that being even higher up in Cusco (3400 m...) than normal would be no problem for any of them!

Twenty gentlemen, quite young for the most part, some with mustaches, looked at me with certain mischievousness. They sat down at little school tables. At first, they were curious about my origins. The simple mention of Cameroon worked like a magic trick: to break the ice in Peru, just say the word "Cameroon": for them, it immediately connects with soccer.

The achievements of Cameroon's national soccer team – the "Indomitable Lions" – seem to be known all over the world by soccer fans, and Peruvians are indeed big soccer fans. A few weeks earlier, I was in Huanchaquito by the sea near Trujillo.

Much to my surprise, the street kids, with whom I spent an afternoon, knew the names of all the players of the Cameroonian national soccer team playing in international teams. They also knew the names of all the players from the 1990 and 1994 World Cup teams. With the kitchen staff, the conversation therefore took off around this fascinating subject.

Then I was able to quickly digress to talk about the few players I knew on the French soccer team, world champion in 1998. It was a good way to start the workshop. And suddenly they looked less mischievous. Funnily, knowing about soccer proved that I was worthy of being taken seriously.

On this note, I introduced the project to them, explaining that they were going to create a "character" who would be Peruvian – and a bit Cameroonian at the same time if they wished!

I had prepared a selection of African and Peruvian fabrics in the kits that I provided. It was up to them to choose. They had forty minutes to create their "character" and then twenty minutes to talk about the experience all together. I had in front of me the attentive eyes of people accustomed to following instructions and being immediately responsive.

They listened quietly to the explanations, and they pointed out to me that they were quite accustomed to manual activities. I asked them to turn off their cell phones and to avoid taking selfies during the workshop.

No one commented: they seemed happy to have this break, ready to take part in this activity, and to momentarily slow down from their frantic work life. They knew each other well, and had fun at the beginning of the workshop, making jokes comparing the material among them: fabrics, threads of wool, beads... I had carefully chosen the word "character"; they told me that they agreed to participate in this workshop because no one from outside was there to observe them.

"If this poses a problem for you, you are free to not participate." This remark made them laugh. For them, there was no way they were missing this experience!

They responded unanimously: "Don't worry. Peruvians like to talk. We are curious and honored."

The subject was closed, and silence quickly fell on the room. I had put on the music from a Zimbabwean artist Oliver Mtukudzi (2). It is relaxing and danceable music and some of the participants started moving on their chairs to the rhythm of the music, all while being completely absorbed in the creative process.

Meanwhile, someone went and picked up the chef. As he came fifteen minutes before the end of the workshop, he asked if he could work by himself to finish his character while we discussed.

Discussion:

The first remarks presented a level of surprise, especially concerning the amount of time designated to the workshop: "I thought I wouldn't have time to finish but I realized that even if I took my time to do everything, I was going to finish on time!"

On the creative process: "I didn't think I could do it," said several of them. I told them how impressed I was with their creativity and the care they put into their work. They puffed out their chests, saying, "Peruvians are great artists", which I truly believed.

Their laughter was filled with gratitude, which convinced me that this workshop was a real experience for them and that it had offered them a trip to a country whose landscapes they only, individually, knew.

With African pearls and cowries, one of them made a bracelet, telling us that these pearls were not found in Cusco and that he was going to make people jealous. He had indeed placed the pearls with great care. Others told me that they were going to do the same, having deliberately not used pearls and cowries for their characters.

When the director came to pick them up, the chef said that he wanted to invite me to dinner that very evening on behalf of the whole staff to thank me for "this magical moment" that they had all just experienced.

I will never regret having climbed so high to hear this.

To be holy,
one must have eaten.

Ful proverb Cameroon

VI – PROFESSIONAL DEVELOPMENT WORKSHOP

With teachers

A few years ago, a commercial appeared regularly on several American television stations featuring a father asking his three-year-old son for permission to take sick leave.

A voiceover replied that a father was not allowed to take a sick day. We are tempted to draw a parallel with the situation of teachers, at least in terms of the expectations that families and society sometimes have of them.

What most teachers (primary school teachers) I meet talk about is the stress they face - a feeling of exhaustion that they have from time to time.

In sum, they share the impression of not doing enough or of doing too much for results that are difficult to measure and that are sometimes unpredictable when face with fixed objectives.

Calming this stress can be linked to the weight of the moral and ethical responsibility of a profession with high responsibilities in a society that evolves with its children, who also must evolve in the existing era to which they aim to adapt as well as they can. Another reality is that parents are often unavailable to their children.

It's important to also talk about the reign of the internet and social networks accessible even to very young children. A teacher told me that he was called "old-timer" by his students because he does not use Twitter. Another shared his dismay at hearing a conversation between two kindergarten students about their Facebook profiles.

- "When I think about it, it just seems like I have no choice but to have one! How do I talk about the subject with them...?"
- "Who are we now and what should we do?" asks another teacher.

The stress has accumulated: it is visible and palpable.

Where and how can you find the resources to continue to do your job well in a world whose evolution we have little control over and in which, paradoxically, answers are expected from teachers? How can one manage relationships with overbooked parents, "over-mediatized" children and an administration that juggles the requirements of the Department of Education and new educational standards? We are far from the image of Epinal from last century of the strong schoolmaster who is in full control of the class with his power, his integrity, and his knowledge.

35 teachers joined me for a day-long seminar. I proposed a project during which groups of five teachers would sit at the students' desks and had to create dolls by inventing a story, that of "Miss Plastic".

Me: "What do you see?" Teachers: "Hangers."

Teachers: "What should we do with it?"

Me: "We will create ladies and gentlemen with clothes made of plastic bags, different types of paper and/or pieces of fabric."

All the materials were laid out on a large table. I had previously asked the teachers to bring with them any kinds of accessories that they would like to add to their dolls. Before starting, they first had to organize themselves and share the materials they brought with one another. There was at first of confusion tinged with annoyance at first. Some would tell me at the end of the seminar:

"Usually for professional development seminars, all the kits and materials that we are going to use are ready for us from the start so that we don't waste time."

"I know that. But today I give you the opportunity to choose and share. All these elements are different: you have to organize yourself so that everyone has exactly what she or he needs. Is taking the time to share and consult on the choices to be made so that everyone is satisfied a waste of time?"

As you can see, everything started well. Everyone had to create:

- A Miss Plastic
- A young Mr. or Miss Paper
- A couple; Mr. and Mrs. Plastic
- A Mrs. Fabric.

When Miss Plastic appeared with face and hair, and dressed in plastic bags, the story of the great changes in the life of Miss Plastic could begin...

Transmission of creativity, from one table to another, from one group to another, through words and gestures: some showed off their latest creation. It felt like a real classroom full of excited teenagers. Of course, creating this series of characters consisted of several objectives that the teachers discovered as their work progressed.

Relaxation and fun, because once the first doll was made, the teacher/student was no longer in unfamiliar territory: she/he knew how to do it, she/he could improve her/his work and add fantasy. The process of repetition was not seen as a loss of time; rather, it was part of learning.

Then comes **repetition** and patience: finding pleasure in doing, granting oneself the ability to be even more creative. There was also a feeling of pleasure involved when these dolls began to take shape one after the other, or simultaneously depending on how each group worked.

Together, each group began to write the story of these plastic ladies and gentlemen:a story for the class based on environmental issues, with their 5 dolls dressed in their clothes.

Here is one of the stories written during the workshop by a group of teachers of Elementary Classes (1st to 5th grade).

Miss. Plastic

The Story of Miss Plastic

Every day, it becomes more and more difficult for Miss Plastic to find plastic bags to make new clothes.

Today, she is invited to a party, and she wants to find plastic bags in different colors to make a nice dress.

She rushes to the stores she usually goes to, but everywhere she gets the same response:

"We no longer give out plastic bags."

"But since when?" She panicked. "Will this last long?"

To find the answers to these questions, she visits her friend Miss Paper who looks very sad and tells her that the only thing she will find from now on are very ugly brown paper bags.

Miss Paper

"I can't find good paper for my clothes anymore. Fortunately, there are still newspapers and magazines, but I heard that they are going to stop producing them to save the trees and the forests and to preserve the air that we breathe."

"I don't understand. There are no trees or forests involved in the making of plastic bags, right?" replies Miss Plastic, almost relieved.

"I know that paper production has been reduced to try and save the trees and forests that humans critically need. For plastic, it's even more serious because the plastic in the bags we find in our stores is made from oil so it isn't biodegradable."

"What does biodegradable mean? Come on, tell me!"

Mr. Plastic

Mrs. Plastic

Miss Paper then starts talking about global warning signs, climate change, CO_2 levels in the atmosphere, the 7th continent of plastic - things absolutely unknown to Miss Plastic, who understands nothing about it and who remains stuck in the fact that she has an important party to attend and needs new clothes. In despair, Miss Paper, who nevertheless wants to help her, says to her:

"Listen, go see Mr. and Mrs. Plastic. I know they have supplies of plastic bags and maybe they can better explain it to you. I realize that everything I say to you must seem boring and nonsensical."

Miss Plastic runs to visit the Plastic family.

Mrs. and Mr. Plastic are very nice people and very concerned about their environment. They know that it's not easy to change everything in a single day, but for several months, they have been using fewer and fewer plastic bags, using only the ones that they have left from their old life. Together, they try to convince Miss Plastic to do the same. They patiently explain to her what biodegradable means and why plastic is bad for the environment, and how it contributes to global warming and the destruction of planet Earth. They tell her about the plastic continent that has formed in the Pacific Ocean and which is now called the 7th Plastic Continent.

"Okay, so I'll go live on the 7th continent of plastic," Miss Plastic says in response.

The Plastic couple looks at her, dismayed and discouraged. How can they explain to this young person the consequences of the multiplication of plastic that we find everywhere, not only in the form of plastic bags? And what about the terrible consequences such as the pollution of the oceans whose fauna could disappear?

"And then, can you imagine that the 7th continent of plastic now has a surface of 1.6 million km2, which is alittle less than half of the European continent? With ocean currents, plastics turn into small particles, which fish and birds mistake for food.

You see, you couldn't even recover pieces to dress yourself! It is urgent - it must stop because other continents of plastic are already forming, not to mention all the mountains of trash that have begun to rise in several countries around the world.

*What counts is not the mere fact that we have lived. It is **what** difference we **have made to** the lives of others that will determine the **significance** of the life we lead.*

Nelson Mandela

Mrs. Fabric

Annoyed, Miss Plastic goes to visit Mrs. Fabric, a very elegant lady recognized by all for her knowledge and charisma. Because she is beautiful and elegant and because she looks at her with kindness, Miss Plastic listens to her. Mrs. Fabric tells her that she has a sewing studio where she can come and sew clothes made of silk, linen and other natural fibers. She can go there now to have a pretty dress ready for her evening party–silk, linen, and natural fibers. Impressed, Miss Plastic doesn't dare ask any questions.

"I'm busy and you want to have a nice dress for tonight, so get to work! I invite you to come and see me tomorrow. I'll teach you about all the natural fibers that will allow you to sew nice clothes. If you want, bring your friends along. It's very important to know all these things. You will better understand the disastrous effects of plastic on our environment."

She smiles at her kindly and continues:

"It's not easy to understand all at once. Don't worry, when it becomes clear to you, you can explain it to others.

At the end of the seminar, the 7 groups told me about what was important during the day. The educational messages had been heard. They also noted several other points:

- The gratifying impression of having taken time for themselves, of having been able to take a break.
- Their tension has decreased: creating these dolls was like reclaiming a part of childhood.
- Inventing a story amused them a lot - it was a real breath of fresh air and increased their self-esteem.

This day was experienced as a pause in time that the elation at the discovery of one's creativity made very special. It was so easy for them to trust one another.

This opportunity that was given to them to work without preliminary instructions initially felt like a burden, but then it transformed into a real challenge of giving life to these dolls: Miss Plastic, Miss Paper, Mrs. and Mr. Plastic and Mrs. Fabric!

Everyone left with their dolls and their stories, free to use them to illustrate future lessons, to continue to create new characters and to write new stories...

VII – A JOYFUL LEARNING PROCESS

"Hello, I speak French": an introduction to learning French with elementary school students.

Learning a language means making room for everything you don't know and that you must approach with humility and curiosity, while experiencing the joy of discovery.

I worked with small groups of students at an elementary school in Manhattan. I divided a class of 20 into 2 groups that I supervised simultaneously. I also encouraged all of them to use words they learned in French or Spanish when they met, making the excitement stronger, because they were under the impression of knowing words that the others did not. The challenge was to remember some words, even while "jabbering through" the rest of the sentence. Having succeeded in memorizing is the beginning of acquiring knowledge, leading to a strong competitive spirit among the learners of a new language.

1 - A bag, with all the materials to be recycled by creating "characters" that will come to life by saying words and leading children into situations requiring more and more words until they develop some vocabulary.

In the bag were threads of wool, pieces of fabric of different sizes, elastic thread, beads, three or four shaped hangers, 2 or 3 rolls of toilet paper, and 1 small plastic bottle. This first kit had all the necessary materials for three afternoons during which we would learn:

- Different parts of the face
- Different parts of the body
- Different members of a family

These puppets would come to life to help advance in the acquisition of vocabulary. We would also use them to meet the members of a traditional family: grandparents, parents, children, uncles, aunts, and cousins. Learners were asked to be very creative because, of course, by using recycled materials, the adults and children of the same family come to life with different basic materials.

Using rolls of toilet paper, the children created cousins with tiny plastic bottles and uncles and aunts with bigger plastic bottles. With each new word and phrase that would come up, the children's hands were involved, "creating" the word before even naming it.

2 - First kit: we must create a person - a man, a woman or other. At all stages of creation, we must speak and respond with a short sentence:

"What do you want to do?" "I want to make the head."

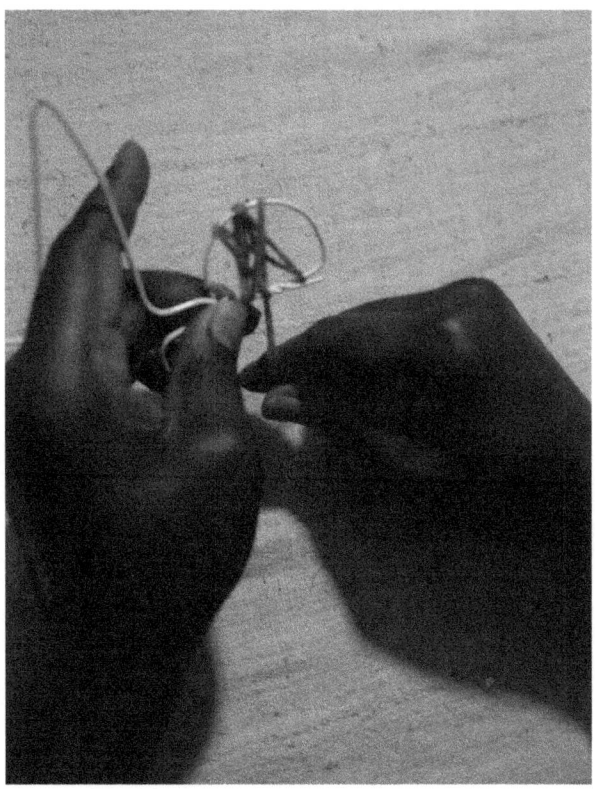

"Now what do you see?" "I see the head."

After a first "family member" was created, the student had to repeat the same steps with words to create the second "family member" with different materials, then go on to make a third one.

Each set corresponded to two or three weeks of learning, 45 minutes per session, twice a week. The time we took to create contributed to the learning process. The acquisition of language is done patiently; each word is received as a gift. During our conversations, the same words were repeated - not in a boring way but each time in a new form, parallel to the work of the hands, and at each step we take.

There was no rush, no urgency. New words were discovered as we created. We didn't see the word until we had created it. The word "hair," for example, came when we had put our pieces of wool on the head - only then did we name them "hair". We took possession of the word "hair".

"What are you doing?"

"I am making the head."

"I am making the hair."

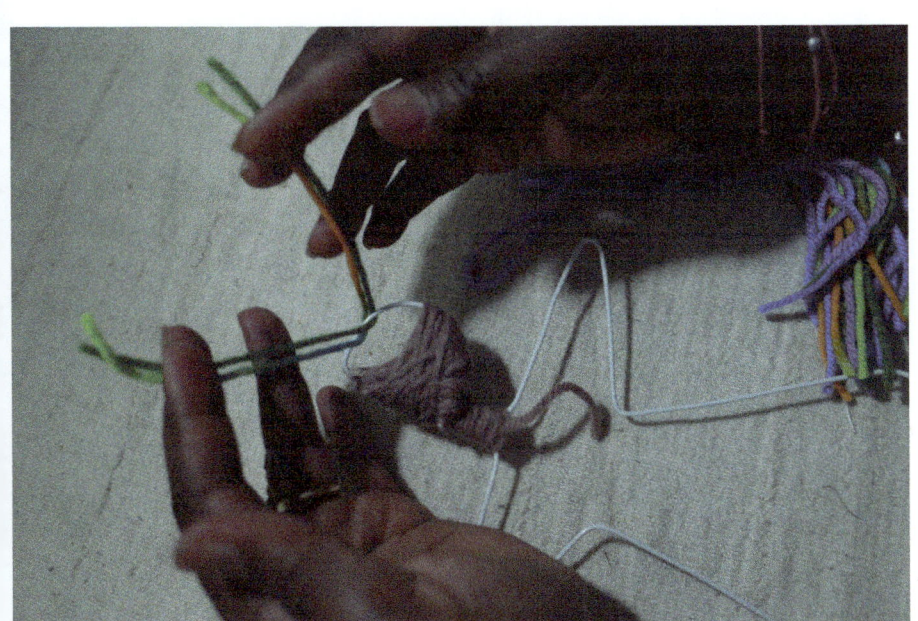

"I see the hair."

"What do you see?"

"I see the head; I see the hair"

Whatever the language studied, we followed the same process. We created, we named.

I made the head. I made the hair.

I made the neck. I made the arms.

I made the body

I made the legs, the feet.

The words would come and go. I stood in the middle of the group. We were learning French. I entered the circle, greeting everyone: "Hello"

They all responded: "Hello."

There was always silence during the creative process. The hands needed the space to be empty of all noise. But when I asked them the two questions:

"What did you do?"

"What do you see?"

Then their tongues became eagerly untied. Sometimes, they responded all together or in just one voice - but, either way, there was no more silence.

Before the end of the 45 minutes spent together, there was laughter when one of the children took on a French accent like the ones heard on television, or whenever there was a lot of "gibberish" when someone tried to tell a story with newly learned words. All without exception retained the seven key words of the day's lesson: the head, the hair, the neck, the eyes, the nose, the mouth, the ears.

- *Take your time:* the time of creation.
- *Favor playing:* we make our puppets dance, we dance together.

- ***Provoke laughter:*** by mimicking what we see but cannot yet name, we mimic what we can't say until we can use the words we have just learned.

- ***Having fun within the repetition:*** we are working on the face of the doll. During these games, other words will be discovered. It is no longer seven words but eight, nine, ten, eleven words that are needed to complete the set of those we already know: eyebrows, eyelashes, cheeks. And there you have it! Without searching for them, eleven words in our treasure box. Tomorrow, or next week, we will have to repeat and practice these words again.

To end a class, I tell a short story in French using a puppet and sometimes I stop to find a word that the learners are supposed to know in a way that, without being asked, they complete the sentence with the missing word.

Beginning of the Pandemic

The Hummingbird Project Message

"The possibility of having fun is an important element in facilitating this transition back to life."

2020. The new Covid-19 virus turns the world upside down. In these strange times when social distancing is the new norm, it's important to contribute on our scale and make lasting changes in our society to save our planet – like the Hummingbird from the Native American legend carrying a drop of water to stop the fire.

So, here is a new creative challenge to help us preserve our human sense of solidarity: the proposed workshop aims to start a global movement that can improve the quality of our lives by restoring the usage of this small object called "a plastic bottle."

Let's take a break, during which the hands return to their primary role: to recycle and recreate.

With a simple plastic bottle taken from our garbage bins, let's create a special doll – "Madame Chiffon" – using anything we can find in our homes to recycle as her clothes (newspapers, old pieces of fabric, threads of wool, beads, etc.).

Everyone can make a "Madame Chiffon": adults, children, alone or together. Let's use this downtime to (re)create. Have fun and relax with this creative project that other people around the world are also working on. Once finished, send the photos of your "Madame Chiffon" and we will display them all at some point, to celebrate life.

Indeed, what could be more insignificant than these small plastic bottles present in our daily life? We found them everywhere during our travels. They are everywhere in the world, on land and in the oceans.

Some make a business out of them by repurposing them to earn a few extra cents. Indeed the bottles can be used to store different products that are sold in markets. In Peru they contain seeds. In Africa, these bottles are filled with palm oil.

And then, one day, they end up in public dumps and other landfills in Indonesia, India or Madagascar...

Sometime before the Covid-19 pandemic, I had proposed with the Alliance Française in Trujillo to organize at one of the two major shopping malls in the city, "Le Real Plaza", a recycling workshop to raise awareness of environmental issues among people who come to shop on Saturday afternoons.

A small, half or completely empty plastic water bottle is so quickly forgotten anywhere in the mall...To do this, I installed tables and chairs in the middle of the mall on which I left a few pairs of scissors on the tables, some glue, pieces of fabric, newspapers, and magazines. Participants in the workshop had to come and sit with a plastic water bottle that they had been drinking from. The workshop ran from 1 p.m. to 5 p.m.

That afternoon, more than a hundred people – parents, children, young people – followed one another and created their "Madame Chiffon."

I remember this 9-year-old girl who arrived carrying a large plastic bag:

"I cleaned the mall," she told me very seriously, showing all the "treasures" she had picked up while walking through the mall, which gave her the right to take over her own large table to create her large "Madame Chiffon".

Let's also talk about a grandmother, who didn't move all afternoon, bent over her "Madame Chiffon" and who asked us: "What are we going to do next week?" How sad it was to respond that I was just passing through for one afternoon. She was discovering a fun way to recycle and spend part of her day.

What can I say about those sixty kids aged between 10 and 12 to whom I proposed the "Madame Chiffon" project and who did not stop smiling throughout the duration of the workshop: a real ray of light that brightened my day. This took place in a school in a poor district of Matara in Sri Lanka.

Certainly, we are living in a peculiar period, where social distancing (6 feet) is the new standard to be respected. For me, it is important to stay spiritually connected if we cannot touch each other. The photos and testimonials of the people who made a "Madame Chiffon" have been flooding in my inbox from France, Peru, Japan, Sri Lanka, the Maldives, Senegal and Manhattan, Brooklyn, and Queens (New York).

Creating a "Madame Chiffon" goes as follows:

To create your "Madame Chiffon", make sure you have the basic materials:

- newspapers and/or magazines,
- an empty plastic bottle,
- scissors,
- white glue, or even a glue stick,
- some tape,
- scraps of fabric,
- colored pencils,
- all kinds of beads,
- sequins,
- and rhinestones.

If you have sheets of paper of different colors or even gift-wrapping paper, all of this can be useful to you.

Be creative even in the different materials you choose to use. Creativity is the keyword. Your mom and/or dad can help you. It's a collective activity.

Adults can make their own "Madame Chiffon" as well, from an empty plastic bottle, or they can simply assist their children.

Project: (re)use a plastic bottle to create your "Madame Chiffon"

It is a privileged moment: everywhere in France, Peru, Japan, and Sri Lanka, children and adults will work simultaneously on the same project and thus remind us that all together, we are the world, we are united...

Very important:

Send a picture of your completed dolls to
myhandsmytools@gmail.com

1. Similarly, the project can also be done starting from a roll of toilet paper. Crumple a large sheet of newspaper or magazine in both hands to form a small ball.

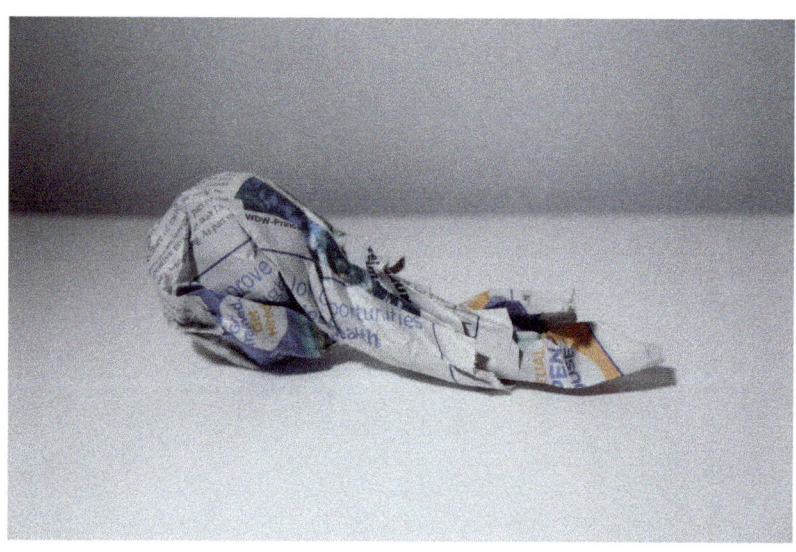

2. Wrap the ball in another newspaper or magazine page and add some thread.

3. Incorporate the thread into your bottle. Do this by turning slowly without crushing the bottle, which must keep its shape.

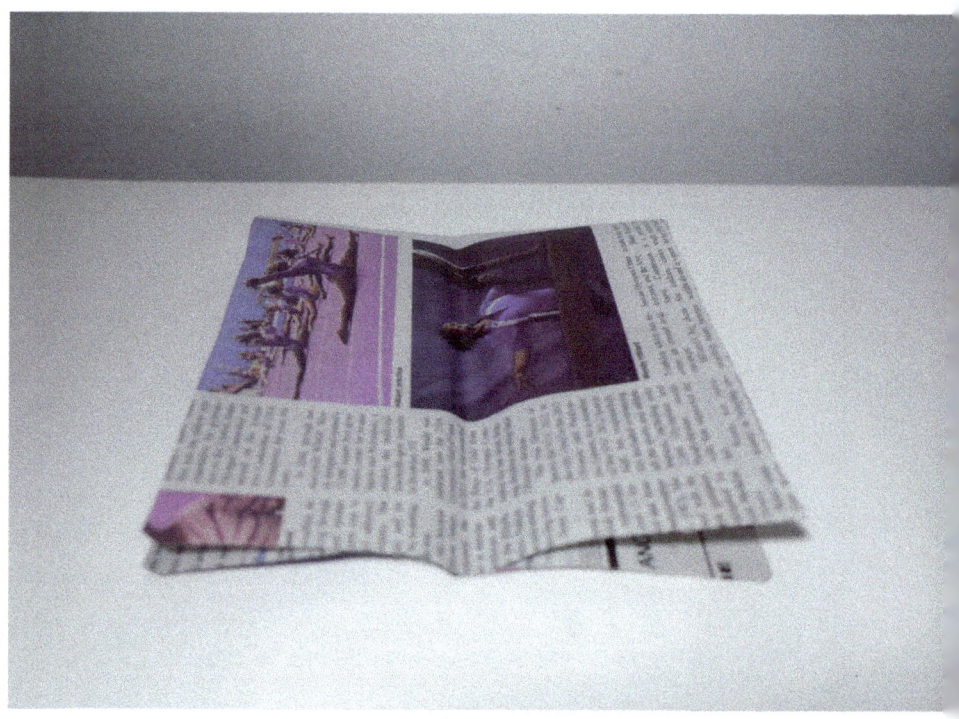

4. Fold your sheet of newspaper or magazine to form a dress. Cut according to the sizes indicated 9" = 23cm wide, 8" = 21cm high. Cut in the middle the required size to put the head through.

Now that the head has been placed, put on the dress: now is the time to be creative.

Consider adding hair, drawing or creating a face, adding arms.

Use all the materials you want to make your doll a very special "Madame Chiffon"!!!

Some testimonials

"Activity shared with the family that allowed us to forge links between generations. For me, it was a question of making the simplest but most elegant doll and using everyday materials (coffee filters, ends of tablecloth, flowers from the garden and my jewelry). Finally, a moment of relaxation and pleasure!"

- Odette C. Dean, Alençon – France

Maxence M. – **4th grade student**

"Friends forever"
written on the fabric he used. Dampiris – France

The Hummingbird Project 95

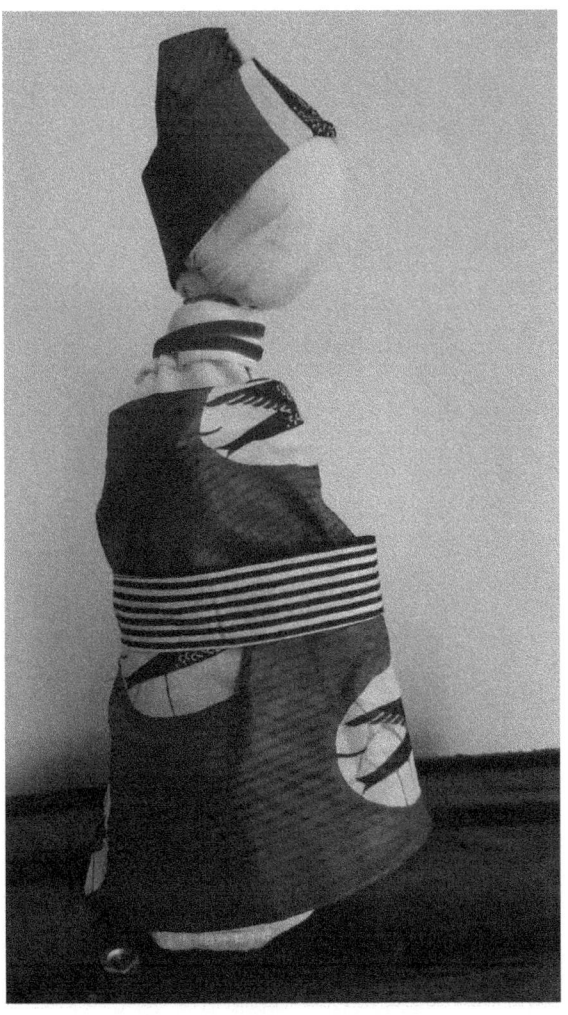

Aurore W. Dakar/Senegal Science Teacher.

"I loved being pregnant and pregnant with twins...my doll lowers her head...looks at her belly...Promise of joys of sharing laughter and hugs with these two little beings to come...Blue because we all love this color...Swallows because I hope my twins will always come back to their first nest, here...So many things in this doll..."

Dialogue between **Inès W.** 6 years old and her sister **Adèle W.** 4 years old; Paris, France:

1. "Great! we're going to make a doll!"
2. "How can we make her arms and legs?"
3. "In a book I saw that for the body we take a bottle."
4. "And the head?"
5. "We'll ask mom!"
6. "Let's just put her in doll's clothes"
7. "Yes, that way she will be beautiful!"

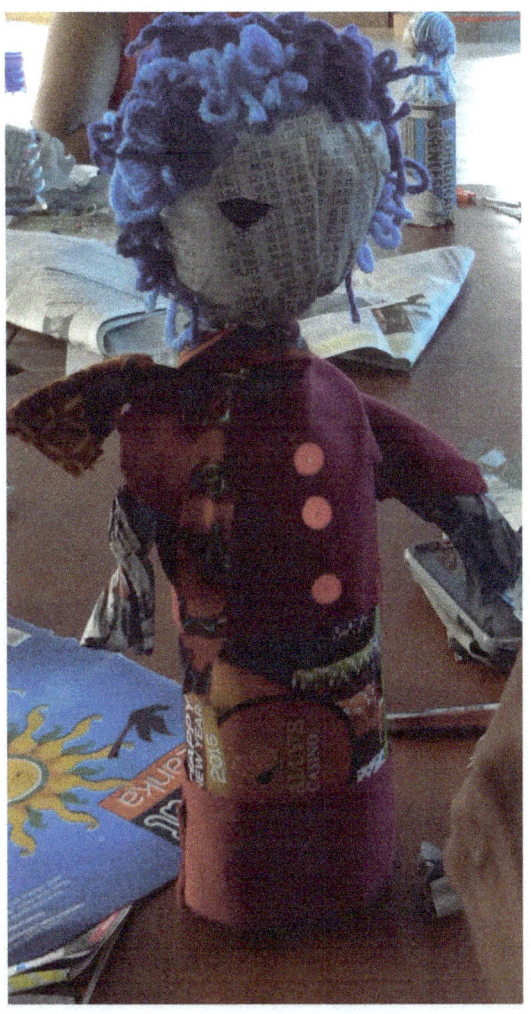

Yenna B. Teacher at Montesorri School, Colombo, Sri Lanka

"Thanks to these plastic bottles, my children and I spent an afternoon of laughter and creation together."

Official Start of the Pandemic

March 2020: Official start of the Covid-19 pandemic. One of the schools at which I had been working regularly since the beginning of the school year suggested that I include the Hummingbird Project in the online teaching program.

Certainly, I was inundated with different information and restrictions: the directives of the Department of Education, the numerous restrictions and the trial and error of the school administration. The latter were looking for solutions so that the children could receive an optimal education and, although it was difficult for me to clearly communicate my wishes both about working conditions and adequate pay, I accepted, happy to be able to support the children.

The Hummingbird Project was therefore part of the curriculum during the last two terms of the 2020 school year in of "Specialists" group (P.E., Theatre, Science, Music, Spanish, Art) at a primary school where I was able to continue to work with three 3rd grade classes, and two kindergarten classes that I had been meeting with regularly since September.

Like many people at that time, my experience of distance learning was quite limited. I had particularly not anticipated the arduousness of the schedule I found myself caught up in.

The 20-to-30-minute work meeting of the Specialists' group every morning at 8 am was just the start! Very quickly, in addition to weekly meetings with all the school staff and the principal, the supervisory staff had also set up meetings for students and parents who wanted to reach a teacher from the Specialists' group. In other words, it was supposed to be sort of a "Zoom office" wherein we could meet with students for forty-five minutes, four mornings a week.

During these forty-five minutes, we had to "receive" parents and/or students to answer their questions. On Friday mornings, I would visit an entire class online on a pre-arranged schedule for a brief discussion with the students and their teachers on all sorts of topics. It was hard to get the kids to talk behind the screen. So, I would tell them a little story and talk about what I had been up to during the week. I'd try to make a joke to make them laugh. Among other tasks, I had an important mission: to call the families of a class that was assigned to me each week. I oversaw the calls during the week under the informal supervision of a group of six to seven people from the administration that I called the Leadership.

The 8 to 10 calls I had to make every day to families would sometimes multiply when I had to answer questions from certain families, forcing me to call them back several times, or when I came across voicemails from people who had to be called back if they did not answer my messages. One of the goals of these frequent calls was to talk to the children and update all the information and documents on the Google Drive so that they could have everything they needed to learn from a distance...

My art and recycling projects had to be submitted to the Leadership before being posted to the children on Friday at 3pm, for the two kindergarten classes and the three 3rd grade classes. The children would discover the projects on Monday mornings and had to submit them to me on Friday mornings.

My research to prepare the weekly projects took me a lot of time because I wanted to make sure that they would offer these young children moments of relaxation whenever they chose to complete them during the four days given to them. When the project was finished, they had to send a photo via Google Drive or directly to my email address created by the school. I also offered the option of sending the photos to my mobile phone, which seemed to make life easier for some parents.

In view of everything that was asked of everyone, students, teachers, and parents, the start was not a walk in the park. As contacts progressed, we discovered the difficulties of some and the bitterness of many. This situation was unprecedented.

How to proceed without any reference point to adjust to? Who to complain to?

The school was busy providing the necessary computer equipment to each family that had expressed a need for it. An IT helpdesk was then set up, available by appointment for both teachers and families to respond to all adjustment and operating problems. Several families panicked while the children adapted quickly and easily to this new situation: it was just a new life to live. Each child had left school with a satchel full of school materials: notebooks, sheets of paper of different colors, blank sheets of paper for drawing, colored pencils, a pair of scissors, a stick of glue, and a reading book as well as all the books necessary for mathematics and language classes.

Teachers remained under pressure most of the time until the end of the school year. The parents I was able to talk to on the phone also seemed overwhelmed by these new norms of life with impacts and changes that were difficult to process.

Many had to deal with sometimes very stressful professional activities (working remotely or having to go to work in person). Several admitted to me that they initially chose to put aside certain questions posed by the online teaching of their children.

The management of daily life had also been turned upside down (during the school year, many children leave the house in the morning and do not come back until the middle of the afternoon. They have their afterschool snack, lunch, and sometimes even have their breakfast there). Now it was also necessary to organize all the meals at home every day of the week!

"The kids only think about eating!" an exhausted mother told me.

It is clear that the mothers as a whole, even those who worked full time, were exemplary and valuable. Often during the day, children were entrusted to adult members of the family (grandmother, aunt, or big sister), but their mothers supervised their daily life. Sometimes when I called single-parent families, I spoke to these women about their place of work.

After several questions and verification, they gave me a number to call to reach their children. These mothers back home supervised the schoolwork, helped the children, and when I asked, they bought the materials needed for our workshops. A mother even asked me if it was possible to provide her with a list of the necessary equipment for her child a week in advance so that she had time to buy everything on Saturdays, the only day when she had a little time to make purchases that she could not entrust to the grandmother, who in turn watched the children during the week. She didn't want her daughter to fall behind the rest of the class.

The language barrier also arose for Hispanic mothers – often, the children were the only ones who spoke English. I translated and posted the projects in Spanish and spoke in Spanish to the Hispanic mothers. To my delight, several mothers also expressed their desire and later their pleasure to participate in my projects with their children!

I therefore went from meeting with children once a week at school for 6 months to meeting with them on Zoom when I joined their classes once a week and from time to time in the "Zoom Office," where three of them visited regularly to talk about the progress of their projects. It was as much a new and confusing experience for me as it was for them: it was as if we were making our way through a video game for the first time.

The Hummingbird Project had to reinvent itself and adapt to a crisis that was destined to last. I started to explore different possibilities to better communicate positive energy to the children: to "ease the tension".

The question of the material was not the least demanding: during my workshops in schools, I usually bring my recycling kits along to make the 45 to 60 minutes spent with the children more effective, even though I have always insisted that a large part of the material can be found at home and that they needed to ask their parents, but few children did. This time, they didn't have a choice – they had to start "exploring" the possibilities they had in their house to find objects to recycle for the projects I assigned to them.

Asking my Kindergarteners and 3rd graders to be creators without knowing what materials they could have at home, without having to go out, was a challenge that brought me back to the very essence of the Hummingbird Project: "recycling and giving new life to discarded items."

Question asked: Were parents willing to let their children search through cupboards and closets? If they hadn't rushed to have fun with all the "treasures" they had in the schoolbags offered by the school, some of this material could also constitute a good basis for working on our projects. The rest depended on what everyone had at home and on a few extras that I asked the parents to buy, very inexpensively, as we had agreed to do with the principal. My selection has always been made in "99-cent" stores.

"99-cent stores are the cheapest stores in the world" (my 3rd grade students said so). In addition, there are many of them across the neighborhoods, and they have never closed, even at the very beginning of the pandemic.

To relax our students, who are used to being taken care of, sometimes excessively, by their school system, what I tried to put in place starting with the first project was a kind of contract of trust between parents/students and myself:

- "Children, I am giving you this project because I'm sure you will be able to carry it out with everything you can find at home and what your parents will buy for you."

- "Parents, please give your children the opportunity to seek and find things that we could recycle together or that could be used in the projects we give them."

Subsequently, I ensured that the proposed projects were feasible with readily available materials and objects found at home.

Communicating with the families allowed me to answer the questions and meet the needs of the children by adjusting the projects so that the challenges had meaning for them.

"Challenge" had become what I called my projects after one of our 3rd graders said, laughing, during one of our telephone exchanges:

"Right now, all your projects are real challenges!"

I repeat, I wanted above all for these projects to become a moment of relaxation and quiet breathing for the young students.

I insisted when they told me they did not have the "required" equipment: I tried to convince them to be "hummingbird students" who always had to do their best in all circumstances and know how to find solutions to cope with any given situation.

I then took up the metaphor of the hummingbird from the Native American legend that, despite its small size and the taunts of forest animals larger than it, flew from the river to the fire consuming the forest to throw the drop of water it carried in its little beak. "I'm doing something, I'm doing what I can." This also became our slogan: Above all, don't stay idle. "I'm doing something, I'm doing what I can."

The children found themselves in front of virtual images of the teacher and their classmates, facing a screen that "monitored" them through the teacher's voice without being able to approach them physically.

To make matters worse, connection problems, poorly connected headphones, and unstable Wi-Fi added to this absence of contact. All this was not easy to manage for children for 3 to 4 hours every day!

I thought, relieved, that they could work off-screen on my projects. When I asked them if the situation was stressing them out, some of the 3rd graders answered that it was "fun" but most spoke to me of "tiredness." They were used to screens, video games in the virtual world, but until now it was always for entertainment. Today school was virtual and some days it was quite tiring or even destabilizing. Not being able to find class friends, to talk or even bicker, they missed it a lot, and part of the exhaustion came from not knowing when it would all end.

Surprisingly, the students who seemed to lose interest in the workshops when I came to their class were among those who had participated most actively in the various workshops and were undoubtedly among the most creative! Certainly, they needed more time than our weekly 45 minutes in their class.

The Hummingbird Project allowed students to showcase their ingenuity, resourcefulness, and ability to make choices. In the classroom, I brought them the equipment, ready to use. At home, to carry out their project, they had to "investigate", be curious, improvise, find solutions, and dare to do. All of this made them hummingbirds, which, following the example of the legendary bird in times of crisis, acted and did their best. It's interesting to see how many of them took up the challenges that I proposed to them: more than 80% of all the projects were completed and at least 3 projects out of the dozen I had proposed initially.

- They learned to be open and creative with what they received and to find additional material.

- They learned to share their work with their moms, their dads, and their sisters and brothers.

Reviewing all their achievements, I'm almost surprised to see that they were able to face most of the challenges offered and still have fun with them.

In this time of lockdown and social distancing, the Hummingbird Project gave children the opportunity to be creative using recycled materials. I also wanted to pursue one of my missions: connect them to the world. They maintained contact with students from a 3rd grade class in Burgundy, France, with whom they had been in contact since the beginning of the school year. I made sure to answer them when they asked for news about their French friends.

I showed them the photos of the "Madame Chiffon" dolls, also made with plastic bottles by Selena, Lola, Ines, and Maxence at the start of the pandemic, and A. suggested that we send them photos of the dolls that she and her mother also created.

"I know they also have distance learning classes, but maybe their teacher can show them."

They asked me if Julian was still doing DIY and if Chloé was still collecting rainwater to water her garden. They also asked me to review the list of challenges for the month of February, received at the end of January and which had started to inspire me.

Challenge of the month of February:

Do manual activities with recycling: Margaux – Inès Y.

Walk to a nearby place instead of driving: Chloe

Remember to turn off the lights when leaving a room, to not leave devices on sleep mode, but turn them off completely: Noah – Tony R. – Lola – Léane – Mathéo – Evan – Florena – Maxence

Use fewer sheets of paper: Inès B. – Estelle – Lilia – Ethan – Tyméo

Use consoles less, and favor instead playing board games or reading books: Tony M. – Inès B. – Tyméo

Consume less water, remember to turn off the tap when brushing your teeth, washing your hands, washing dishes, press the small flush button: Nashwan – Léane – Mila – Séléna – Lily – Paul.

Pick up litter in nature: Martin – Noa – Lilou – Julian

At the DIY workshop, with plastic bottles that we were no longer using, we prepared a game of chamboultout – we decorated and painted the bottles. Chamboultout is a game where you line up the bottles, like in bowling, and you throw a ball to knock everything down (you can put outdated newspapers in a used sock to make the ball, for example).

I did not want to confuse them by talking too much about the past. I also took the opportunity to tell them what I had not been able to tell them in class for lack of time!

This letter reached us long after. I sent it to the principal, and I would read it to those I would meet at the start of the next school year:

Dear friends of La Cima,

After all these months, we hope you are well.

Do you remember? We started our correspondence before the Coronavirus pandemic and we would very much like to resume it, perhaps at the start of next school year.

It's good to have been able to get to know each other and we enjoyed our exchanges of letters and photos where we were able to talk about our holidays - you about Thanksgiving and us about our Carnival. You remember, we wrote you a letter in English; it was a lot of work but we are happy to have done it.

Thank you so much for the big envelope you sent to us that we were able to discover when we returned to school in September that had a bit of your life at La Cima inside: your flyers, your badges and more.

We had also received before the lockdown the "Madame Chiffon" project, the dolls to be made with small plastic water bottles. This made us want to try as well, so, during the lockdown, some of our classmates made dolls with materials that were going to be thrown away: bottles, string, scraps of fabric...and sent you the photos that we hope you received.

We also hope that you have received the challenge that each of us set ourselves for the month of February: to implement eco-gestures to better protect the planet and take care of it (such as, for example, taking less baths, watering the garden with rainwater, reducing waste, etc.). We would love for you to give it a try too.

It would be really great to continue our correspondence and maintain our bond even though we have never met so we look forward to hearing from you.

Cheers.
Paul, Julian, Tony, Martin, Ethan, Noah

For each project, I read a short paragraph on an environmental subject followed by a question they had to answer in two or three lines. Very few answered all the questions, and there was rarely anything elaborate or any research...Obviously, the questions and discussions we had in class were not fully able to advance their knowledge and, above all, to arouse their curiosity. Their curiosities were visibly more stimulated by the project to be created.

However, on Wednesday, April 22, 2020, Earth Day, without any request being made to them, T. wrote:

"It is important to celebrate this day because we live on an Earth we share. That is why it's special. We must celebrate the Earth every day, and dedicating a day to it helps remind everyone of our duties towards nature because we must also express our gratitude for all that the Earth gives us."

That same day, several wrote to us that they wanted to "do good things for the planet" and that using recycled materials found at home was one of those good things to do for the planet!

These class hours were weighed down by the attention required to be able to follow the teacher. Games and relaxation were also necessary. In addition to a few pages of reading that their teachers requested, how could they expend additional energy to go surfing on Google and search the National Geographic site for information on the environment? It wasn't impossible, but it was certainly not amusing!

Quarantined or not, through television, they could hear words that intersect with the readings I offered them, such as bad weather, climate change, stratospheres, virus, deforestation...

It was therefore important to address these subjects, which are an integral part of my creative projects. But I limited the requirements to what they agreed to write to me.

Let's review some of their lessons and how they carried out their projects.

Let's follow A., who asked his mother to photograph the different steps he took to create a doll with a roll of toilet paper and a doll with a plastic bottle:

- **Step 1**

I gather everything I will use: two toilet paper rolls, an empty plastic bottle, threads of wool, a ping pong ball, newspaper, white glue, pieces of fabric, colored ribbons that my mother gave me, pieces of rhinestones, markers, and colored pencils.

- **Step 2**

I create the head of the plastic bottle with a ball of newspaper and cover it with a construction paper sheet.

I create the head of my toilet paper roll by wrapping the ping pong ball in construction paper.

- **Step 3**

I dress my two dolls with the pieces of fabric, and the ribbons, trying to use what I have on my table plus what my mother kindly added.

- **Step 4**

I take the time to work on the faces one after another. I place the hair, and I draw the eyes, the nose, and the mouth. For my doll made with the toilet paper roll, I also add arms that I made out of construction paper.

S. in my kindergarten class had to decorate a large flower and its leaves with collages. Having no more sheets of paper of different colors, she tried to paint the flower and leaves herself. Certainly, helped by her mother (who later confirmed she did), she also used tissue paper of different colors.

The choice of paint to give an impression of collage came from her, her mother assured us.

For the project *I protect my city with my name*, the three 3rd grade classes had to use graffiti, like street artists, to draw their first name, behind which they had to add buildings.

C. didn't have color pencils at the time of the project and worked on a series of very elaborate black, white, and gray graffiti as well as the buildings behind his first name, while J. created a whole composition between the buildings and his first name by playing with the colors. Neither forgot their self-portrait as a signature. Well done, artists!

Working online required primary classes to be well organized. If we wanted the students to be able to find answers, we had to provide them with information that was easy to manage and understand to avoid them becoming overwhelmed.

My main challenge was making sure that the child/student was able to relax. Why not be "scattered" and get off the "beaten path"? I'm not naive enough to claim that the students were able to assimilate and understand everything, but I took care to remain simple my the presentation of the projects to be carried out, reminding them to always take the time to look around themselves and discover what will allow them to be creative.

The Hummingbird Project in Times of Covid-19

Our daily lives continued to adjust to the rhythm of the pandemic with all its mysteries and questions. While a return to school was on the horizon for some establishments with face-to-face teaching, others continued teaching remotely or in "hybrid mode" – these new words were now a central part of our vocabulary. The usual meeting places, as well as the doors of museums and libraries, remained closed.

I took advantage of this time offered by the circumstances to work on my creations. I asked a filmmaker friend to put together an exhibition or even a film project. The idea was to make dozens of my big dolls dance in the air in an allegory of freedom from the stress that had accumulated over the recent months.

Although very reduced in number and duration, my workshops were not systematically canceled in schools. But I had to show a lot of resilience to justify my interventions and to convince administrators of the obvious: my workshops were necessary, as were classes in dance, drawing, painting, and all artistic disciplines. I patiently explained that artistic education could help and limit the different types of withdrawal into oneself that are dangerously looming amidst this pandemic.

I thought of the Native American legend of the two wolves. We all harbor two wolves within us: the dark wolf that pushes us towards evil, anger, envy, hatred, and fear – the fear of dying from the Coronavirus, this fear that plagues everything, today and tomorrow.

And then there is the other happy and resilient wolf who pushes us towards the light and the good. In the battle between these two wolves, the legend says the winner is the wolf we feed. So I proposed to help feed the wolf of goodness by giving students the opportunity to be creative...I remember a screenshot of a 3rd-grade class: 20 faces of attentive children, focused on what they were drawing. Their teacher pointed out to me:

- "It's extraordinary! I rarely see them so attentive."

The legend of the two wolves is about the power of attention and mindfulness.

I was forced to cancel the shipment of material kits to be distributed by certain schools because some parents, fearing too much handling, did not want them. There was not much to answer when it came to ensuring the safety of children and reassuring families, even if it meant endorsing all sorts of phobias, but I refuse to make any judgment here.

Would YouTube become our ally? Should I, like many, throw have thrown myself into this adventure?

I continued to doubt it – not so much the effectiveness of the videos, or the dozens, even hundreds of "views" that would reassure me, but far from satisfying me, what came to my mind were the words of a song by Charles Trenet whom I like very much:

What remains of our loves?

What remains of those beautiful days? A photo, an old photo,

From my youth.

Faded happiness, hair in the wind, Stolen kisses, moving dreams.

What remains of all this? Say it to me...

...Again and again, screens and isolation...

The Hummingbird Project, while maintaining its "recycled arts and environment" status, would make up for the lack of art classes in the school where I worked during the first period of the pandemic. The students' schedules were relieved of "non-essential" subjects.

So, there were no more art classes, and my intervention was reduced to a contract of 4 sessions per month for the 2 classes of each level in rotation during the school year: i.e., 4 times 45 minutes for each live class every month.

Meeting children live made them closer. I quickly got over the frustration of spending so few hours in person with the children during the school year. I chose the option to shorten the time required to complete the project. One after another, each child presented their work and spoke. It was a voice that came through the screen and reached me, an energy received that I could respond to.

Whatever was said, the important thing was these words that come out of the screen. The exercise, which lasted only two short minutes, was the same for all classes from kindergarten to 5th grade. Some students sometimes tried to extend these two minutes by getting lost in long descriptions. I stopped them with a kind word because I had to move on to the next one. In any case, this allowed each child to communicate directly with me and the rest of the class and truly take ownership of their work.

The "I did it" affirmation was essential and brought students back to the reality of the work being done. A face, an energy transmitted, a voice that I would help to relax when I felt a little tension.

"It's very beautiful what you did...and all these colors, it's wonderful..." "I can't really figure out what you drew...can you explain to us what you did?"

The student/child would then gladly agrees to revisit his/her creation with us. These minutes of communication were precious.

One day, I stood, curious, at the "door" of a 3rd grade class in its second school year of "distance/online learning". I listened to what the teacher said:

Monday morning.

"Hello friends, glad to see you again! I hope everyone had a relaxing weekend. It is 8:30 a.m., we are meeting on Zoom. Well done, I see everyone is here. It's important to be on time. Remember that at the end of the day, you have to do your homework on Google Drive. I also remind you that you have to read for 30 minutes every night! Before we start, I would like to remind you of several important points:

- *I see that you are all wearing your uniform shirt. I hope you are also wearing appropriate clothing below: just know that when you get up, everyone can see you entirely on the screen.*

- *If you haven't already, I'll give you 5 minutes to find a quiet space to work, and don't forget your headphones! You must also have the notebook of the day, a well-sharpened pencil, and white index cards.*

- *Also, try to have your reading and science workbooks as well as your math workbooks placed near you.*

One last thing, don't forget to use Clever to log into Raz Kids, DreamBox, Typing Club, Amplify Reading, and Google Classroom every day!"

Wow! I was impressed! After a day of class navigating between Raz Kids, DreamBox, Typing Club, and Google Classroom, students could use a long period of relaxation. I imagined for these six-year-old children a workshop/recreational moment with all kinds of games. I would give them space to run and then sit on a bench and talk about what they did during the day. They could then gently make fun of their teacher, who bored them with long to-do lists.

I imagined a workshop where speaking would be free and come out of the screen...

A Hummingbird Project in Ambohitra - Madagascar

For several years, I have been holding a workshop during the month of the Francophonie with French students from a private high school in Manhattan.

The French teachers with whom I was in contact shared with me about their fatigue and that of their students and the difficulty of setting up a creative workshop, with some of the students attending the course on site and the other half attending online on Zoom.

They offered to have me play "the interview game," answering questions about Ambohitra, the Hummingbird Project I have been involved with for several years. Talking about our relationship with the inhabitants of Ambohitra, a village on Sainte Marie Island in Madagascar, and thus giving students the opportunity to enter this village that was almost unknown to the world seemed to me to be an interesting subject for students very stressed out by the pandemic.

Ambohitra is a set of three villages about two kilometers apart, with a total of 750 inhabitants. No one ever goes to Ambohitra; only the inhabitants move out of necessity to the large towns of Sainte Marie, a very touristy island.

A few days before I came to speak, the teachers with supporting maps presented Madagascar, also called "La Grande Île", to their students. Located in the Indian Ocean, Madagascar is one of the 54 countries of the African Union, independent from France since June 26th, 1960.

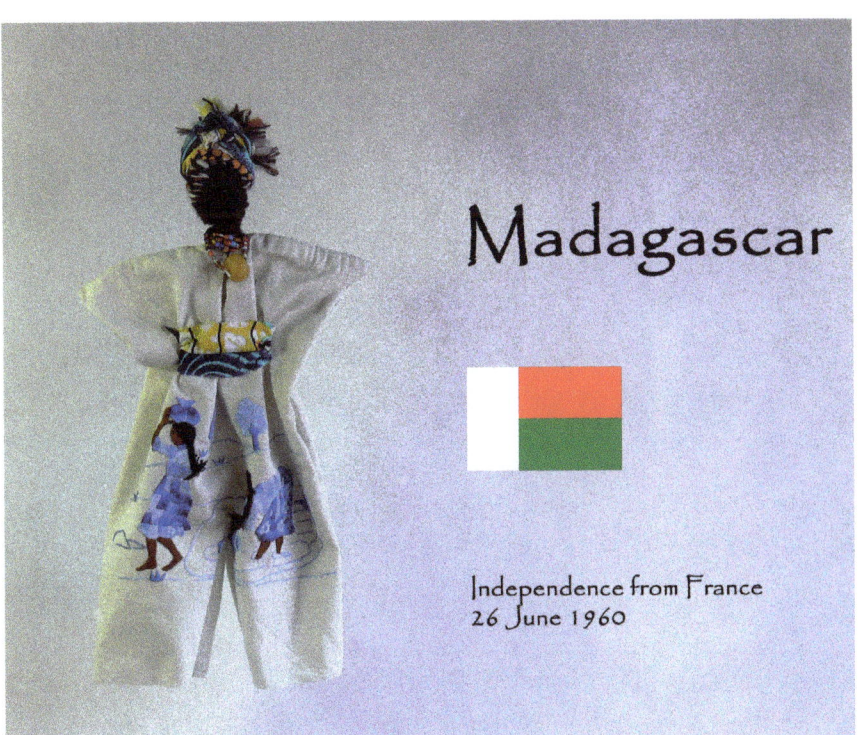

The friend who told me about Ambohitra, Yolande C., was living, at the time when I met her, in Pornic (France). She is a midwife and therapist. In fact, she only began to speak to me about Ambohitra after the terrible hurricane Ivan devastated Sainte Marie Island and the villages of Ambohitra on February 7th, 2008. At that time, Yolande created a non-profit with some friends to help the inhabitants of Ambohitra called the Nosy Mitarika Association (the Island Association which guides Nosy being the Malagasy name for Sainte Marie Island, the flagship island).

Indeed, none of the aid and donations sent to help Sainte Marie reached Ambohitra except for a few tents offered by UNICEF so that the children could remain safe and continue a formal education.

Yolande regularly visited her mother at Sainte Marie. She told me later that every year during her visit to Sainte Marie, she used to meet very young girls from Ambohitra who had come to attend their first year of college; they were pregnant and were also carrying babies in their arms. Yolande began to think about ways to create a safe center to prevent these young girls from sometimes being housed in conditions that exposed them to the sex tourism that was rampant on the island. This center would welcome them, protect them, and prevent them from becoming easy prey to abusers.

For now, the most urgent task was to rebuild a primary school because as the years passed, the UNICEF tents got torn. No matter how much the women patched them up, they became unsanitary and no longer protected the children from the weather. Unfortunately, the funds allocated for the reconstruction of the school were partly misappropriated by officials from the Ministry of National Education.

Buildings had been rebuilt with cheap and flimsy materials; toilets had been ignored altogether. The association's work was therefore to allow teachers to work in decent conditionsand to take care of the construction of a building with rooms to house the teachers.

Most teachers lived on Sainte Marie Island, about eight kilometers from Ambohitra, and if they couldn't sleep there, they had to get up at 5 am to come and teach.

Since the education of children was also a priority for my organization, My Hands My Tools then joined the actions of the Nosy Mitirika Association. With about thirty photos, I told the story of Ambohitra and the great work accomplished by the men and women of the village. I even found the photo of the Certificate of Recognition issued in 2015 by the Ministry of National Education, a subtle transfer of payment for the salaries of the 5 temporary teachers. Apparently this certificate officially authorized the Nosy Mitirika Association to build a school and take care of its proper functioning!

All the people of the village started to work together, putting aside all their old quarrels and resentments, which made it possible to progress well on all the projects. During each visit of the members of the Association and others, all the inhabitants of the village gathered and met over a festive meal. Thus, very strong bonds were formed, and there was greater awareness of an important responsibility concerning the village.

Yet, since 2008, many members of the Nosy Mitarika Association have abandoned the work, and many friends of My Hands My Tools advised me not to get involved in this project that was too big for me, emphasizing the fact that it was difficult to fight against corruption coming from above but also from the dignitaries of Sainte Marie.

The hummingbird flies from the river toward the fire and back without hesitation. It was about doing what I could: even the Covid-19 pandemic hadn't stopped me. I decided to move forward with the people of Ambohitra while continuing to convince others to join our project because, of course, the hummingbird will not extinguish the fire alone, but through his efforts and energy, others will join forces to help put it out.

We can change things with our voices, our hearts, and our hands. The only condition is that we never stop as long as we can breathe and can move!

During this day, more than a hundred students listened to me. At the end of my presentations, the same two questions were always asked:

- What are your top priorities in Ambohitra?
- What can we do at our level to be hummingbirds?

"To be hummingbirds?" I shared some of my reasons.

First, how can we abandon these children who do not even have the possibility of making their toys with materials to be recycled as we did during our early childhood? We were, at the time, in my great-grandmother's village, in Ebolowa in Cameroon, experts in creating toys with a stick and tin cans. Of course, environmentalists would say it's actually good news if one cannot find anything to recycle in Ambohitra: not a cardboard box, not a plastic bottle, nothing but the surrounding nature and the thousand treasures it has to offer and which I would like to explore with the children of Ambohitra.

Besides nature, as you can imagine, they also have their own soccer team!

Physical education is as important for children's education in Ambohitra as anywhere else. The kids are very sporty, run and walk fast, play soccer, and have become champions of petanque (after balls were gifted Ambohitra's young soccer team a few years ago).

Some time ago, there was a women's team that everyone would like to see come back. Accompanying children to Tamatave (3) for sports competitions is no easy feat, but many mothers strive to do so. The trip is veryexpensive, so they take pots and food supplies for the road and travel all the way so that their children can take part in the competitions.

Among the projects already in place, several are to be continued. In particular:

- In addition to the school buildings, a classroom still needs to be built quickly for the many preschoolers. Once their school education is taken care of, it will free up the young mothers who will be able to go to work.

- There's a need to build a vegetable garden and grow vegetables there, and regularly bring them carrots, potatoes, and other plants to improve the children's diet based mainly on rice.

Madagascar is known for its biodiversity. Yolande pointed out to me that while walking in the abundant vegetation surrounding the villages, she often picked up herbs that are safe for human consumption. The presence of a naturalist would help the village feed on what can already be found there and overcome fears based on many ancestral prohibitions that limit the consumption of certain plants that they do not know. I imagine that a young naturalist could settle in the village for a few months, study and list all the plants that make up the richness of the country.

- The pandemic has intensified the precariousness of the village because the luxury hotels of Sainte Marie were emptied of their tourists. Therefore, the women could not sell their produce and the men could not find work. Fortunately, everyone's resilience and the few donations received have allowed the children to have a seemingly normal back-to-school experience in 2020-2021. As Yolande told me, the priority is above all that the children receive a meal at least once a day (the costs needed to feed the children amounts to about $300 per month).

- Ambohitra absolutely must keep its teachers. Thus the 5 temporary teachers must continue to receive a monthly salary. These Hummingbird teachers earn a monthly salary of about $52 euros! They deserve all our respect. They sleep in the classroom after the school day until they can be provided with living spaces when they are too tired to go home.
- Yolande also promised to go and have a firm talk with the people from the "high-ranking" ministry, as they are called – whom she knows – to solve the problem of the teachers' salaries. It is time for the government to take this situation seriously.
- I repeat: the education and well-being of children is everyone's priority in the village. The women of Ambohitra refused to allow their little girls to have to walk several kilometers every day in the morning and evening to and from school in Sainte Marie, the risk of rape being too great. Elementary school through 6th grade is as important to their integrity as it is to the education of children.
- Another priority concerns the sanitary conditions: the children regularly build large panels with Ravenala leaves (3) to protect the bathrooms, but over time it creates sanitary problems. Therefore, the construction of toilets for children and teachers is more and more urgent.

- The inhabitants of Ambohitra discovered the television. A large TV had been given to them: it works for 2 hours every week and allows the whole village to watch DVDs which I've been bringing to them. However, there is a problem: the TV requires a power supply which makes purchasing a solar panel an urgent need. In fact, I have made it one of my main priorities!

Yes, the task is enormous, but solidarity is not an empty word.

To tell the story of Ambohitra, the village and its inhabitants is not to make a list of what is missing but to speak of a contract of trust and sharing. All expenses are itemized. From a cybercafé in Sainte Marie, I communicate with Michael, the director of the school, whose charisma impresses me. A bank account has been opened for the residents who work together to distribute the money received.

The correspondence with Michael is sometimes difficult because he's not fluent in French. He speaks mainly Malagasy, like all the inhabitants of the village.

I had an agreement with the Alliance Française de Sainte Marie to offer French lessons to teachers; it's been on hold for a while, but that too, should resume soon. French is spoken everywhere in Madagascar: it is the main language of communication and, above all, a professional language. These inhabitants of the tip of the Phare Island live in total instability but are not miserable.

Unknown to many, forgotten by their own government, they work, take care of their children and seek solutions for their lives. They participate fiercely in discussions on the future of their children. They fight to take care of them and themselves despite having no medical coverage. For me, it has become so necessary to accompany them.

It's the obvious truth that I can't possibly second-guess...

Another Hummingbird Project...Mancey

A few years ago, I spent a few days with my childhood friend who lives in a little village in the French countryside in Burgundy.

My friend and her husband imagined that I lived in the Wild West, completely disconnected from real life as they conceived it. So, they made it a point of honor to have me eat fresh fruits and vegetables from their garden, as well as eggs from their chicken coop and cheeses from their neighbors' goats.

For a few days, I dove into their universe of simplicity and good flavors. I pointed out to them that in New York, I eat tomatoes from my bed (5), and cook with the basil and mint I grow in my community garden. I also explained to them that there are farms in New Jersey from which I receive excellent fruits and vegetables!

A little higher, a little further.
I want to go even further.
Perhaps higher up I will find other paths.
It's beautiful, it's beautiful.
If you could see the world down there, it's beautiful, it's beautiful...

Jean-Pierre Ferland

© Arièle BONZON / Le Réverbère Gallery, Lyon France

One Thursday, when I was at their house, they offered to take us to "the bistro" – the local bar/restaurant. Surprised, I asked, "why are we going to the local restaurant when we have everything here?"

They explained to me that this week, Le Bistrot was to take place in the garden of Gerard M., where tables have already been set up. I ended up spending a fantastic time among these people I did not know. Several images intertwined in my head: my block in Harlem, where people from several buildings, mostly adults, meet in the evening and organize barbecues. I never asked myself if it was legal. In any case, no one has ever been kicked out, even if the smoke from the barbecue sometimes bothers the inhabitants of the neighboring buildings.

I also thought of those exhausting afternoons when I was leading workshops with the seniors of the NYCHA community centers (6). I felt their need to relax, but I came up against the difficulty of erasing their accumulated frustrations due to an unwanted loneliness and all the limits that stood before them each time they thought about what they were going to do tomorrow or the day after. So, their expectation was enormous, and their attitudes would become quite aggressive when they didn't get what they asked for.

These bistros would be a wonderful idea for sharing, but no one had ever told them about this possibility or suggested setting up friendly meeting places. Let's listen to Gérard M. tell us the story of their "bistro," a project set up "just to be together."

A brief history of Bistrot Mancillon

Mancey is a village of 400 people located in the region of the vineyards of the south of Burgundy, 100 km from Lyon, the third largest city in France. The particularity of this village is the dynamism of its inhabitants.

You be the judge!

During the summer of 2016, a dozen residents met at each other's home several times to think about what they could do together to enliven the village. Among the ideas put forward: the creation of a village bistro.

Traditionally a bistro is a place that is both warm and modest where you can discuss everything and nothing while having a drink, sharing a simple dish or a snack. There are bistros everywhere in every city in France, but they have unfortunately disappeared in many villages due to the rural exodus and evolving lifestyles. In the past, before the war, there were at least three cafes in the village, one in the town and two in Dulphey. In Mancey, the need to meet in a friendly way, around a table, remains. It has been felt for years.

When the members of the small group all agreed on developing a friendly meeting place, the proposal had yet to be made into something concrete. Fortunately, there is still a restaurant in Mancey, "l'Auberge du Col des Chèvres", located in the premises of a former café-restaurant in the village, once run by the famous Vonette (7) and her husband.

In this very place, there is still a coffee nook with tables and a sort of bar. But the owners only operate it as a restaurant every day between 12 p.m. and 2 p.m. during the day and between 7 p.m. and 9 p.m. in the evening. It was not very difficult to convince them to open the small room adjoining the restaurant to welcome people once a week, on Thursdays between 6 p.m. and 8 p.m. for those who wish to revive a café in the village. The name chosen by the inhabitants to symbolize this revival was "Bistrot Mancillon"(8).

An appeal was sent to the population and very quickly a core of regulars formed – about twenty people, men and women. From the very first meetings, the discussions had around one or more bottles of Mancey wine (or fruit juice) and snacks of all kinds brought by everyone, focused on the activities that could be launched within the small group.

Some proposed to organize board games: tarot, a card game very popular locally, belote, quizzes on French songs and singers. Others preferred to focus on different subjects: unusual objects brought by different people, the cultivation of tomatoes, the history of the Château de Mancey, the collection of old coins, soup competitions, the patois of Mancey, fishing techniques, the tales and legends of Tournugeois...

But from the very first meetings, the main activity of the bistro was to discuss village life: current projects, problems that arose, or events affecting families (births, deaths, illness, departures, and arrivals, etc.). The participants became very loyal, even if each week the numbers could vary between 7 and 25 depending on everyone's personal schedules. For many of us, Thursday evening was the occasion for a theatrical outing in Chalon organized by the Table Ronde, the cultural association of Mancey.

The most popular activity at the Bistro Mancillon (7) was undoubtedly the meals organized in the dining room next door: the end-of-year meal, of course, the start-of-summer meal, before the holiday closure in July and August, and the birthday meal of our Dean Georges, who is over 100 today. During these meals, we eat (well!), we drink (of course), but we also sing and tell stories. We even had joke contests, a custom deeply rooted in popular culture in France.

The Auberge also concocted a meal for us with "Jean Ducloux", the famous creator of the Greuze restaurant in Tournus, known throughout the world.

In 2017, upon the arrival of a marquee in the village with a theater troupe from Nanton, the friends of the bistro organized a wine tasting, with a presentation by the former director of the cellar of the winegrowers of Mancey. The musical entertainment was provided by a musician from the village. The evening ended with dancing.

In 2018, within the bistro, we organized a theatrical performance on the theme "the history of bistros through the ages in Mancey." Several of us have participated in the writing of skits: one having a Gallic village as its setting, another an inn from the Middle Ages, and the last a tavern being set at the time of the French Revolution. The members of the Bistro played the different characters, and the children of the village came to join them. For many of us, the preparation period for the show, which lasted 4 months, has remained a highlight in our collective memory. The performance took place under a marquee with more than 100 seats, erected on the town hall square. The inhabitants of Mancey turned out en masse to see the show, which was greatly applauded.

The following year another play was presented under a new marquee with the help of the Round Table, the cultural association, on the day of the Village festival, with the same success. The theme this time was "the television news through the centuries" – at the time of the witches in the Middle Ages and always at the time of the French Revolution.

During the summertime, we decided on a change of scenery. Every week in July and August, on Thursdays at 7 p.m., we organize a "rotating bistro" at each other's homes.

We would meet outside, often in a garden. Each participant would bring some drink and food in a spirit of true conviviality. These summer meetings took place in the four hamlets of the village: in Mancey-Bourg, Dulphey, La Bussière, and Charmes. Everyone was happy to share their lifestyle with others.

In the bistro, we organized an outing to the magnificent Bibracte museum, located near Autun. We learned many things about the inhabitants of our region before the Roman conquests. It was also an opportunity to share a "Gallic" meal at the inn located next to the museum.

Our weekly meetings continued at the Auberge until our 2019 end-of-year meal. Then the Auberge closed its doors due to the illness of the owner. We organized a birthday meal for the 99th birthday of our dean in Tournus.

Then came the lockdown and its constraints...

During the summer of 2020, in the period of temporarily lifted lockdown, we brought the Bistro "at the inhabitant's home" back to life. But it was then forced to sleep for health reasons.

But like the phoenix, the bistro will soon be reborn and perhaps in a new location: it is, in any case, one of our village's projects for the future!

Description of Some of the Videos that we Propose

1 - Create "people" from hangers

I create people from all over the world with hangers salvaged from dry cleaners. "Creating people" is one of the workshops we do most often at the request of schools.

I have been working in a primary for about ten years in Westchester (New York). When I introduce my programs to teachers, this project is always the top choice. Several reasons are given for this: notably, brothers and sisters or classmates of the students who created their dolls ask to do this workshop – they also want to make their own doll! The workshop allows children to develop several skills: for the very young to learn knots, for example when you have to put your hair up or tie a belt, It also opens them up to other cultures, makes them curious and more...

Ms. J. one of the 3rd grade teachers:

- "We study the African continent in 3rd grade, bringing them to the Bronx Zoo when we talk to them about wildlife and animals. On top of that, having your program is great because it helps us to study one or more countries on the African continent. It's important to create a doll by making the students listen to the music of the country, by talking to them about the culture, the daily life, the clothes... It helps us a lot. We cover many of these topics, before and after the workshop, and believe me, one of the 'side effects' of your workshop is that they talk about it long afterwards!!"

An African Ninja… and… A Japanese Samurai

... Bursts of laughter!

Indeed, these hangers have often given me incredible surprises.

One evening at the Alliance Française of Trujillo in Peru, I found myself in front of a group of blind adults who had expressed the desire to participate in this specific workshop.

The Alliance Française of Trujillo and its director had already approached me with various challenges: street children, women in hidden residences, and workshops in the shopping mall. At first, although I welcomed this new challenge, I felt very hesitant. Although each blind person was accompanied, I wondered about the right procedure to follow. How were we going to do it? I had never run workshops with blind participants or even learned how to do so.

I took the time to prepare the kits and reorganize them in such a way to facilitate both the helpers' work and the participants' creative process.

- *Shaped hangers,*
- *I wrapped the wool around the heads so that they were ready to receive the hair,*
- *For the hair, I prepared pieces of wool previously cut to be attached to the head,*
- *The garments – skirt or pants, tunic and belt were prepared in pieces that were easy to adjust to each other.*
- *I also added extra pieces of fabric for accessorizing.*

I thought for a moment that I would do this workshop without music, but nothing prevented us from listening to it during the workshop. I therefore chose Seckou Keita, a kora player, and Malian singer: "Who am I? Who are we?" says this modern-day griot.

I quickly noticed that each participant had a helper, either a family member or a friend. A young woman stopped me and asked if I could work with her: she would be alone during the entire workshop because her mother had an emergency and would come back to find her later.

She wore sunglasses and a bright smile:

"My name is Marisa."

"Okay, Marisa, I'll explain how we're going to work, and I'll come and sit next to you."

At that very moment, I experienced a slight apprehension in light of the expectation I felt from everyone and from Marisa in particular.

Participants and helpers worked in pairs. I addressed everyone: the question "What do you see?" – the common denominator of my workshops – remained the same: to see with your eyes, to see with your hands, to touch in-depth to move forward in creation. So, I felt I didn't need to change my vocabulary.

"We're going to make African dolls. I'm going to say what I'm doing with Marisa. You're going to look at us and do the same thing. We're going to move forward, each at our own pace. Do not hesitate if you have any questions."

Then I went to each participant to give them a kit of materials and to let them discover hand by hand what was in the bags.

Time stood still; the attention was extreme.

I repeated the same words and the same gestures as many times as necessary. The notes of Seckou Keita's kora began to land on each of us as if to enlighten us from within.

Creating this doll was done in an almost sacred atmosphere – everyone listened, and then the hands did the job. Caregivers, no doubt accustomed to this support, only intervened in a tactile dialogue.

Marisa broke the silence by asking me with an amused smile.

"You said earlier that you matched the hair to the colors of the clothes. Tell me again what color my doll's hair is?"

"They are blue and green, and I put a little yellow."

"It's perfect! These are colors that I like. Please, I would like a blue fabric for the skirt and a yellow one for the top, if it is possible, of course."

I was convinced Marissa was challenging me: I looked in all the kits I had left. Not for a moment did I want to disappoint her because these colors seemed important for the creation of her doll.

I also agreed to challenge her. When I came back to her, I said to her: "Look, I found what you want."

Quietly, she ran her fingers over the fabrics of the tunic and the skirt.

"Thank you, it's perfect. Too bad if there are other colors with the yellow of the tunic, it doesn't matter, it will work very well."

Time continued to flow in this atmosphere where only the music bound us together.

Marisa finished creating her doll on her own. When she finished it, she presented it to us, waving it slightly with a broad satisfied smile. I was fascinated by the harmony of colors. Marisa is blind: I didn't ask her how and when she lost her vision. I let her continue to surprise me in a luminous exchange during which she told me about her daily life, her studies, and her pleasure in learning French at the Alliance Française.

II – "Knitting plastic bag yarn"

The women of a women's shelter in the Bronx (9), whom I met with regularly, repeatedly asked me to offer them a workshop that they could then transform into a lucrative activity in order for them to make objects to sell.

They wanted something easy to learn that they could make without a big investment because most of them had little money. There was a sewing machine in the common room, but it was hard to come up with an activity in which they could all participate simultaneously on the machine. We offered crochet and knitting to the group's enthusiasm. Most of them liked knitting or crocheting and others immediately offered to teach those who didn't know how to knit or crochet.

Mischievously, I suggested that they create their own thread.
- "Creating our knitting yarn?"

- "We continue to find far too many plastic bags: I suggest you keep them; we will transform them into knitting yarn."

They therefore started to collect, search and ask everyone who came to work at the shelter to bring them back these plastic bags, which are gradually becoming a rare commodity.

We experienced an intense waiting period: the women were so eager to get to work, they told me.

I had brought them some crochet hooks and knitting needles so that the novices could start learning. It had become "a state affair," as they liked to say. For four weeks after our first discussion, each time I arrived, they began by showing me their collections of plastic bags and seemed disappointed when I told them that we needed even more. One day, we were finally able to start cutting the bags to make our yarn, which we packaged in round balls.

The balling revealed their state of mind and their impatience, always on edge. They helped each other: when one was unable to cut a long piece, someone else, with ease, would stop her work to help her.

The bags were not all the same shape, and some lighter plastics were difficult to hold. They then settled in pairs to cut it. This "state affair" was a matter of women and solidarity. Nothing seemed to affect their good mood, their goal being to have at least 2 very large balls. They were busy loudly and joyfully.

We spent the two-hour workshop cutting, tying knots, and laughing – an activity that they made light and playful, punctuated with bursts of joy. Usually always very stressed out and in a hurry to finish whatever they were doing, they had fun like teenagers during our workshops.

Creating this unusual and different thing together made them bond and created a "special" connection. When I was able to talk about them while preparing my work, it was an impression of strength that emerged from their comments: they were "specialists", pioneers in recycling, and whatever they could achieve with these balls of "thread of plastic bags", they were aware of being at the first stage of a creative process that they mastered and could pass on to others.

"One Plastic Bag" - Isatou Ceesay and the Recycling women in Gambia by Miranda Paul

I brought this children's book to these ladies. And it was without a doubt the only book they agreed to read during my workshops, and I had to order several copies to give them one each!

They told me how much they wanted to live outside a system of overconsumption. They couldn't afford it, but above all, they didn't see the point. So, following the example of the Gambian women in Miranda Paul's book was good and very motivating!

They asked me several times if other women in Africa recycle plastic bags or other polluting objects. The idea of meeting other women to start other projects motivated them: They felt ready for these trips. Many items were created: small pouches, dolls, placemats, and this bag they wanted to offer me.

The package tied by hand, the foot will not undo it.

Ekonda proverb Democratic Republic of Congo

III – "My Secret Bag"

I insisted that art workshops remained a priority during this time of a pandemic. Being creative helps children to be resilient and aware of the importance of their place in this world in which they evolve.

One of my projects, "The secret bag", carried out with 2 paper plates and ribbons, seemed to appeal to my young students. I observed two approaches: some students remembered the word "bag" and immediately launched into elaborate bag projects, sometimes very sophisticated. Very few remembered the word "secret" and took the opportunity to pass on a message inside their bag. They wrote down their concern from the moment.

I chose *"The Secret Bag"* of young Mia, 7 years old. She and her family were very affected by the death of Georges Floyd on May 29, 2020, in Minneapolis (10). She chose to create a bag open to all to write these words:

"Every day on the news,
we see this injustice in our world.
Where is the love?
We are all human beings.
It doesn't matter what color our skin is.
It's time to stop the hate and fear and start showing love.
If we remain united, hatred will not pass.
It's time to change with love."

Bag created by a 3rd grade student from La Cima Charter School Brooklyn - New York

IV - Cutting and Gluing

Few questions about the pandemic were asked to me by the children I was in touch with, as if the subject did not interest them.

One of our 3rd grade students nevertheless wanted to tell me about it.

His grandfather, who had spent a few days with them three months ago, had caught Covid-19 and died. So in his family – he continued in a monotone voice – they were all going to die one after the other: first his parents, then his big brother, and soon his turn would come.

He did not seem frightened. His way of understanding the pandemic was in all these bits of information heard on television, such as the assumption that those who the virus had not approached from near or far would survive. In his childhood life, there was constant, hyper-publicized death, recorded daily, and tirelessly commented on by the media. It was no longer a question of life but of death on a day-to-day basis; an amplified death from which he could not escape since it was inevitable for those who had been in close contact with someone affected by Covid-19.

The conversation through our screens did not seem to me the best way to discuss it with him. I notified his teacher. It was a difficult experience to bring a seven-year-old child back to life.

I chose beauty. I called on my Teacher, Henri Matisse, to help me. I opened the door and the windows to the spring which returns, to the trees which find their leaves again, to the sun which shines again to the point of dressing in yellow. Two projects, one for cutting and one for collages and the same subject: Life.

"Keep your eyes closed for two minutes. Imagine a very beautiful place where you would like to live, a place with trees, houses, including yours, the sun, birds, butterflies, flowers too and more things if you want."

With the pages of colored magazines, postcards, greeting cards, and other sheets of construction paper previously donated or found, they carried out one project using scissors and another by tearing the sheets according to the sizes they wanted to get for collages. This gave the power to their hands to make them dream and appropriate these moments of simple beauty during the time of creation.

Total amnesia: it lasted a little less than an hour and through the screen, I observed their faces, their concentration, their attention, and there, some relaxation, the outlines of smiles in front of improbable, unexpected colors.

*Good or bad, there is way too much information.
Many can't take it anymore.
It is good to be able to escape from this influx of
information and allow everything to become centered and
peaceful
when we put nature at the center of our attention.*

*Cut out and collages created by a 3rd grade student from La
Cima Charter School Brooklyn - New York*

For Mia

In recent months, for the Hummingbird Project, each new experience has presented itself as a new journey to be taken by learning to look at a screen to first meet faces and then finally children.

It was not easy at the beginning. Staying within the simple framework of the program seemed to me to be the right attitude to work calmly with the children. It was necessary to quickly detect those who, for one reason or another, head down, installed in such a way that it was impossible to see precisely what they were doing, were dropping out. Those were the ones who, when I reviewed the work of the class, told me with a falsely sheepish look that they didn't have the material, so they couldn't do anything. I also learned to never fail them while letting them breathe at their own pace.

Nothing extraordinary was required of me because, as for all teachers, the situation was unprecedented. Faced with the pandemic, we had to invent, even reinvent ourselves regularly, to be as close as possible to each student on our screen.

I want to express my gratitude to young Mia who visited me four mornings a week from mid-March to mid-June 2020, in my Zoom office. Mia really took care of me: she made sure to keep me alert and strong. Mia, a seven-year-old child, shared her daily life with me and allowed me to move forward, to quietly engulf myself in the breaches she opened for me.

She held my hand.

I walked with her without knowing how to proceed at first but I grew more and more confident as time went on. How to transmit? And what to send? Pointless questions. Thanks to Mia, I understood that in a given space, each individual occupies a primordial place, and that I could feel the presence and the energy of each one by simply asking myself: "What do you see?"

It was no longer a feat, being able to be in a virtual class in which the children did not hesitate to question me, to interact with me in a simple relationship in which I managed to explain the projects to them and then let them work and express their creativity. There were, and of course, there still are, special and magical moments like in "the life before", pre-pandemic!

Because it is often when nothing spectacular is required of us that we come to our senses and move on. So, when we've come to our end...the grace is there.

*"I love challenges,
and I approached the project just like that. To imagine
creating a doll from a small plastic bottle with the material
available at home - to make a doll that looks like a doll
provided pleasure and serenity."*

"Madame Chiffon" by Agnès Violet, Nurse Anesthetist
Dakar – Senegal

Our Readings during the Pandemic

"The workshops take place in hospitals as well as in schools, colleges or high schools, raising awareness of the resources of recycling, in a kind of 'aesthetic pirouette,' which gives all its meaning to the act of artistic creation, in an atmosphere bathed in music, where literature is never far away, near a library."

JJ Beaussou

I took the time to re-read some of my favorite books, and I also had time to read the books I already had but hadn't yet read. The start of the pandemic and the lockdown allowed me to discover many children's books that I read with much pleasure. Then I would show them to my young students during our Zoom meetings. I was in New York at the time of the first lockdown, so a majority of those books are in English. I could not go to museums. However, thanks to the books I could access online, many artists inspired me, accompanied me, and helped me to prepare my workshops.

Books read and reread

Take the time to look, to learn to see...

"Mara had thought the game would never change. But one evening she was there when her little brother was asked for the first time, "What did you see?" then she realized how much the game had changed for her. Indeed, now it was no longer just: "What did you see?" but: "What did you think?" "What made you think that?" "Are you sure that your thought is true?"

Friedman, Samantha: Matisse's Garden with reproductions of artworks by Henry Matisse, Published by The Museum of Modern Art

With Romare Bearden, participants in the "Collages" workshops immerse themselves in a whimsical and fantastic world. With collages that mingle with painting without any distinction, Romare Bearden offers a magical and colorful world.

Mayers-Heydt, Stephanie & O'Meally, Robert G. & Delue, Rachael Z & Devlin; Something Over Something ElseRomare Bearden's Profile Series, Published by the High Museum of Art, Atlanta in Association with University of Washington Press, Seattle

A Fascinating Discovery: Bill Traylor, a self-taught artist born into slavery in Alabama, immediately captured the attention of young students, especially his drawings depicting his experiences and observations of rural and urban life in symbols, shapes, and figures repeated and purified. Our students got to know Bill Traylor and tried to reproduce his drawings.

"In the hands of Bill Traylor" Works from Xaire, 4th grade student

Lessing, Doris; ***Mara and Dann,*** Harper Perennial, a Division of HarperCollins Publishers

Wangari Maathai, our Mama Africa continues to inspire me, a book for third graders:

"It's almost as if Wangari Maathai is still alive, since the trees she planted continue to grow. Those who care about Earth like Wangari can almost hear her speaking the four languages she knows - Kikuyu, Swahili, English, and German - as she does her important work."

Prevot, Franck: ***Wangari Maathai - The Woman Who Planted Millions of Trees,*** Published by Charlesbridge

"A friend agrees to help... Then two... Then five. The women cut the bags into strips and roll them into spools of plastic yarn. In a short time, they learn to crochet with this yarn." I took this children's book to the ladies in the Bronx, New York, and it was undoubtedly the only book they agreed to read during my workshops, so much so that I had to order several copies to offer them! Paul, Miranda; One Plastic Bag - Isatou Ceesay and the Recycling Women of the Gambia, Scholastic.

The genocide of the Tutsi April 7, 1994, in Rwanda: Upright Men workshop with a group of high school students from New York. "So the war between the Tutsis and the Hutus is because they don't have the same territory? The discussion stopped there. It was all very odd."

Faye Gael; ***Small Country***, Hogarth, London - New York

"Gérard the teacher, his life will be saved. And he will one day find our school, spared by the arsonists" Habonimana, Charles; Me The Last Tutsi, Plon

"Matisse got very close to heaven with a pair of scissors." Romare Bearden "Matisse or the apprenticeship of scissors". In class it is an encounter with small hands that learn to

master an appendage called scissors. "A pair of scissors is a marvelous instrument"
MoMA The Museum of Modern Art New York; Henri Matisse: The Cut-Outs, Published by The Museum of Modern Art

Winter, Jeanette; Henri's scissors, Kids SimonandSchuster.com - Beach Lane Books

The Bill Traylor exhibition was held from September 28, 2018 to March 17, 2019 at the Smithsonian American Art Museum Washington D.C. USA

Umberger, Leslie; *Between Worlds - The Art of Bill Traylor, Smithsonian American Art Museum, Washington, DC. in association with Princeton University Press, Princeton and Oxford.*

No doubt because Paul Klee was fascinated by the children's drawings from which he was inspired, his work challenges children who find themselves in his relationship between shapes, colors and music which makes "the invisible, visible".

Duchting, Hajo; *Paul Klee Painting music,* Prestel Publisher

Vry, Silke; Paul Klee for Children, Prestel Publisher

Haftmann, Werner; *Paul Klee, Watercolors - Drawing - Writings, The most Comprehensive Painter of our Century,* Harry N. Abrams, Inc. Publishers New York

Street Art is the history of art on the move. I can have debate and discussions with students of all ages. The students ask me a lot about Street Art. Overall (those of New York) they showed reluctance to talk about graffiti, persuaded to transgress a taboo. Granted, these subversive graffiti began to appear on the sides of train cars and walls, they were the work of gangs in 1920s and 1930s New York. Since then, this illegal activity has evolved into many forms of artistic expression.

Mattanza, Alessandra; *Famous Artists talk about their vision - Aryz- Banksy, Philippe Baudelocque* , Whitestar Publishers. Exciting work.

Danysz, Magda; *Knowing Street Art,* Knowledge of the Arts Editions

Environmental Matters – Elementary Course That Helped Explore Earth and Space, Gareth Stevens Publishing

Benoît, Peter; Climate Change, Scholastic

Bomsper, Pam-Dick Rink; *The Problem of the Hot World*,

Butterfield, Moira; *1000 Facts about The Earth*, Scholastic
Fabiny, Sarah; Where is the Amazon? WHOHQ Who? What Where

Grohoske Evans, Marilyn; *The Bee's Secret,* Pearson Waterford Institute

Heos, Bridget; *It's Getting Hot in Here The Past, Present, and Future of Climate Change.* Houghton Mifflin Harcourt

Kamkwamba, William and Bryan Mealer; *The Boy Who Harnessed the Wind,* Ed. Deal Books For Young Readers

Kentor, Sondra; *Under the Garden Gate,* Heinemann

Marsh T.J. and Ward, Jennifer; *Way Out in the Desert.* Rising Moon

Matero, Robert; *Eyes Nature Lizards,* Kidsbooks

McNeely, Jeannette; *Water,* Pearson Waterford Institute

Polisar Reigot, Betty; *A Book About Planets and Stars,* Scholastic

Ramírez, Carlos; *The Four Seasons,* Waterford Institute

Shapiro J.H; *Magic Trash, A story of Tyree Guyton and his Art,* Charlesbridges

Simon, Seymour; *Global Warming,* Harper

Titlow, Budd, Tinger, Mariah; *Protecting the Planet, Environmental Champions from Conservation to Climate Change,* Promotheus BOOKS

Woodward, John; *Eyewitness Climate Change,* DK Discover more

III - BOOKS FOR CHILDREN

Bennett Hopkins, Lee; *Behind the Museum Door. Poems to celebrate the wonders of Museums,* Harry N. Abrams, Inc.

Bull, Jane; *Make it! Don't throw it away,* DK Discover book

Bolden, Tonya; *The Champ The Story of Muhammad Ali,* Scholastic

Brooke D., Beatrice & Carvalho of Magalhales Roberto; *Art and Culture of the Prehistoric World,* Rosen Central

Burleigh Robert; *Langston's train ride,* Scholastic Caines, Jeanette; *Just Us Women,* Reading Rainbow Book

Cambers, Catherine; *School Days Around the World,* DK Readers

Charles, Oz: *How is a Crayon Made,* Scholastic Inc.

Cuyler, Margery; *Please Say Please! Penguin's Guide to Manners,* Scholastic Press, New York

DePaola, Tomie; *The Legend of the Indian Paintbrush,* Scholastic

Diaz, Katacha; *Treasures from the Loom,* Pearson Waterford Institute

Dillon, Diana; *I can Be Anything Don't Tell me I can't,* Scholastic

Ellery, Tom & Amanda; *If I had a Dragon,* Shimon and Shulter Books for Young Readers

Emberley, Rebecca; *Let's Go A book in Two Languages,* Little Brown and Company

Fenner, Matthew; *On My Block,* Real World

Lyon Jones, Cherry; *"Movin' to the Music" Time,* Pearson

Waterford Institute

Meache Rau, Dana; *We the People, The Harlem Renaissance,* Compass Point Books

Obama, Barrack; *Of Thee I Sing. A letter to my daughters,* Alfred A Knopf

Pope Osborne; *Favorite Greek Myths,* Scholastic

Pwell Hopson, Darlene and Dr. S. Hopson; *Juba This and Juba That, 100 African American Games for Children,* Fireside Book Published by Simon & Schuster, New York

Tarpley, Natasha Anastasia: *I Love My Hair,* Little Brown and Company

Roalf, Peggy; *Looking at Paintings Musicians.* Hyperion Books for Children New York

Shahan, Sherry; *Party. A Celebration of Latino Festivals,* August house

Schunk B. Laurel; *The Snow Lion A Chinese Tale;* Pearson Waterford Institute

Silvano J., Wendy; *Sweater,* Pearson Waterford Institute

Sobel Lederman; *Noah Henry, A Rainbow Story,* TBR Books

Sobel Lederman; *Masks!,* TBR Books

Stojic, Manya; *Hello World, Greetings in 42 Languages Around the Globe,* Scholastic

Yacowitz, Caryn; *Native American Seminole Indians,* Heinemann

Shahan, Sherry; *Party. A Celebration of Latino Festivals,* August house

Wilbourn, Laura; *Asterion's Elixir,* Blurb

Aardema, Verna: *Printing the Rain to Kapiti Plain,* Reading Rainbow Book

Angelou, Maya; *My Painted House, My Friendly Chicken, and Me,* Dragonfly Books

Angelou, Maya; *Kofi and His Magic,* Crown Publishers, New York

Burns Knight, Margy; *AFRICA is not a country,* First Avenue Editions

Chamberlin, Mary and Rich; *Mama Panya's Pancakes - A village Tale from Kenya,* Berefoot Books

Cherry, Lynne, J. Plotkin, Mark; *The Shaman's Apprentice a tale of the Amazon Rain Forest,*

Darrell, Elphinstone; *Why the Sun and the Moon Live in the Sky,* Houghon Mifflin Company, Boston

Dillon, Leo and Diane; *To Every Thing There is a Season,* Scholastic

Edinger, Monica; *Africa is my home - A Child of the Amistad,* Candlewick Press

Feelings, Muriel; *Jambo means hello - Swahili Alphabet Book,* Puffin Penguin Young Readers

Feelings, Muriel; *Moja means One- Swahili counting Book,* Puffin Penguin Young Readers

Gerson, Mary-Joan; *Why the Sky is Far Away - A Nigerian Folktale,* Little Brown And Company

Goldner, Janet; *Obama in Mali. Men's Hair Salon,* Building Bridges Press

Graney, April, *The Marvelous Mud House - A story of finding Fullness and Joy,* BH Kids

Hamilton, Virginia; *The Girl Who Spun Gold*, The Blue Sky Press

Harmon, Ruby M.; *Dromedary and Camelot*,

Haskins, Jim; *Count your way Through Africa*, First Avenue Editions

Markman, Michael; *The Path - An Adventure in African History*, A&B Publisher Group

Marsh T.J. and Ward Krebs, Laurie & Cairns Julia; *We all Went On Safari - A Counting Journey Through Tanzania*, Barefoot Books

McBrier, Page; *Beatrice's Goat with afterword by Hillary Rodham Clinton*, Aladdin Paperbacks - Simon & Schuster, New York

McDermott, Gerald; *Anansi The Spider*, Henry Holt and Company Traditions

McKissack, Patricia and Frederick; *The Royal Kingdoms of Ghana, Mali Songhai, Life in Medieval Africa*, Square Fish

Musgrove, Margaret; *Ashanti to Zulu, African Traditions*, Puffin - Penguin

Ndiaye Sow, Fatou; *Jerejef,* NEAS Collection The New African Editions of Senegal

Oliver, P. James; *Mansa Musa and The Empire of Mali, The True Story of Gold and Greatness from Africa*,

Onyefulu, Ifeoma; *A is for Africa*, Turtleback Books

Powell Hopson and Hopson Derek S.; *Suba This and Juba That*, F A Fireside Book, New York

Romero Steven, Jan: *Carlos and the Squash Plant*, Northland Publishing

Stanley, Fay; *The Last Princess. The Story of Princess Kaiulani of Hawaii*, Scholastic

Steptol, John; *Mufaro's Beautiful Daughters, an African Tale*,

Scholastic Temko, Florence; *Traditional C often rafts from Africa*, Muscle Bound

Thompson, Laurie & Qualls Sean; *Emmanuel's Dream. The True Story of Emmanuel Ofosu Yeboah*, Random House

Verde, Susan; *The Water Princess - Based on the childhood experience of Georgia Badiel*, G.P. Putnam's Sons

Walker, Barbara; *The Dancing Palm Tree, and other Nigerian Folktales*,

Walters, Eric; *From the Heart of Africa, a book of Wisdom*, Tundra

Wisniewski, David; *Sundiata Lion King of Mali*, Clarion Books New York

Music

Music accompanied us during the workshops I presented. It gave us inner peace: inner peace that I'd like to share with workshop participants (adults and children).

An anecdote: Some time ago I worked in the premises of the Alliance Française of Iquitos (in Peru) with a group of about thirty hearing- impaired teenagers. Cello and kora notes invaded the entire space, creating a lively atmosphere despite the silence in which the teenagers moved. I was busy distributing material when one of the teenagers came to tell me with hasty gestures that there was no more music. The director of the site who entered confirmed what the child had just said. It was clear that the vibrations released by Ballaké Sissoko's Kora had worked their miracle.

SOME OF MY FAVORITE TITLES

I advise to always choose music that relaxes us, calms us and makes us feel good. The list below could be much longer because I'm so passionate about opera, so-called classical music, jazz, music from Africa and other places around the world. However I have intentionally reduced the list because running a workshop is a moment of sharing and certain music allows us to communicate and share better. The titles below are those that accompany my workshops most of the time.

- Ballaké Sissoko (all his music) (Kora)

- Ballaké Sissoko Vincent Segal: Chamber Music and Night Music (Kora and cello)

- Seckou Keita - 22 Strings

- Mamadou Diabate - Tunga, Heritage and Behmanka

- Anouar Brahem – Wave

- Toumani Diabaté & Sidiki Diabaté - Jarab

- African Dreams (Lullabies Cradles Songs from the Motherland

- African Dreamland (Putumayo selection of African lullabies)

- Dreamland (Putumayo selection of countries around the world)
- African Lullaby (West African lullabies)

- South African gospels sometimes accompany us, among others:

- Soweto Gospel Choir – Blessed

- Healing Music of Zimbabwe

- Stella Chiweshe - Talking Mbira (Spirit of Liberation)

- Manish Vyas – Water Down the Ganges

- Dave Premal – Twameva Healing mantras

  And for late afternoons with our adult participants:

  - Oliver Mtukudzi all his songs, warm and dancing To sing and play with the little ones
  - 50 most beautiful nursery rhymes

Table of Illustrations

Page 9 – "Madame Chiffon" by Vickie Fremont May 2021 – Photo Dulce Lamarca

Page 15 – The Traveling Penguin, Gift from Antonio, 2015 Workshop at Tecsup Trujillo- Peru Photo Dulce Lamarca

Page 18 – Upright Men Workshop – Achievements of the students of High School Manhattan - New York Photo Dulce Lamarca

Page 19 – Upright Men Workshop – Achievements of the students of High School Manhattan - New York Photo Dulce Lamarca

Page 27 – Upright Men Workshop – Directed by Vickie Fremont for the commemoration of the Tutsi genocide – New York. Photo Dulce Lamarca

Page 31 – ME to MYSELF Workshop New York Upstate – My Twin created by P. Photo Dulce Lamarca

Page 39 – L.'s twin ME to MYSELF Workshop New York Upstate "I fly", Photo Dulce Lamarca

Page 45 – Fashion bag "The day I decided to be beautiful...I stopped having the nightmare that has wrecked my nights for many years..." – Photo Dulce Lamarca

Page 52 – Masks Workshop – Creation of Masks-Elephants Manhattan – Creation of J. one of the participants New York Photo Dulce Lamarca

Page 59 – Men's Workshop, Kitchen Staff - Cusco Creation of a Peruvian character by J. the Chef. Photo Dulce Lamarca

Page 64 – Professional Development Workshop – Group of 35 teachers from 1st. to 5th grade New York – Miss Plastic – Photo Dulce Lamarca

Page 66 – Professional Development Workshop – Group of 35 teachers from 1st. to 5th grade New York – Miss Paper– Photo Dulce Lamarca

Page 68 – Page 69 – Professional Development Workshop – Group of 35 teachers from 1st. to 5th grade New York – Mrs. and Mr. Plastic – Photo Dulce Lamarca

Page 73 – Professional Development Workshop – Group of 35 teachers from 1st. to 5th grade New York – Mrs. Fabric – Photo Dulce Lamarca

Page 77 – A Joyful Learning Process – Learning a language in Elementary Class "I do the head" – Photo Dulce Lamarca

Page 79 – A Joyful Learning Process – Learning a language in Elementary Class "I do the head" – Photo Dulce Lamarca

Page 80 – A Joyful Learning Process – Learning a language in Elementary Class "I do the hear" – Photo Dulce Lamarca

Page 88 – 3 photos: How to create a "Madame Chiffon" – Realization Vickie Fremont workshop offered internationally – New York. Photo Dulce Lamarca

Page 89 – 2 photos How to create a "Madame Chiffon" – Realization Vickie Fremont workshop offered internationally – New York. Photo Dulce Lamarca

Page 91 – Photos How to create a "Madame Chiffon" – Realization Vickie Fremont workshop offered internationally – New York. Photo Dulce Lamarca

Page 93 – Photos received as part of the participation in the international project. Photo from Odette C. of Alençon – France

Page 94 – Photos received as part of the participation in the international project. Photo from Maxence of Dampiris. – France

Page 95 – Photos received as part of the participation in the international project Photo from Aurore W. in Dakar – Senegal.

Page 96 – Photos received as part of the participation in the international project Photo from Helene W. in Paris.

Page 97 – Photos received as part of the participation in the international project Photo from Yenna in Colombo – Sri Lanka

Page 111 – Graffiti created by a 3rd grade student from La Cima Charter School Brooklyn – New York student. Photo Dulce Lamarca

Page 117 – Vickie Fremont archival photo from the exhibition RE... Re-Cycle, Re-Create, Re-Imagine June 2009 – September 2009 at the Museum of Biblical Art New York Madagascar one of the 54 African countries- Photo Yves Leroux.

Page 121 – Photo from 'Ambohitra-Madagascar. The Principal of the Elementary school and his soccer team.

Page 127 – Photo Ariele Bonzon Mancey, 09.21.17 - 2:50 p.m. Extract from: "Tribute to Pierre De Fenoÿl" (Detail)

Page 134 – An African Ninja and a Japanese Samurai Created by Vickie Fremont. Photo Dulce Lamarca

Page 141 – Creation of knitting yarn with plastic bags. Bag donated by the Ladies of the Bronx, New York Photo Dulce Lamarca

Page 143 – Creation of The Secret Bag by Mia. a 3rd grade student from La Cima Charter School Brooklyn – New York. Photo Dulce Lamarca

Page 147 – Cutting and Gluing – 3rd grade students from La Cima Charter School Brooklyn – New York. Photo Dulce Lamarca

Page 151 – Agnes Violet's doll – photo Dulce Lamarca

Page 154 – "In the Hands of Bill Traylor" Works from Xaire 4th grade student. Photos Vickie Fremont

Acknowledgments

I thank:

César Chelala, my Commandant Che, always dedicated to promoting my work, and without whom the book would not have been written.

Professor Teboho Moja who immediately gave me her trust.

Alice Bornhauser my friend who read the first pages, all the way from Orléans.

Marie Allemand, my big sister, and my goddaughter Minnie Sottet, both efficient proofreaders.

Marie Mangeot for having so effectively encouraged me since Fontainebleau.

Yolande Catoire, for her warm presence during the time of writing.

Anne Finkelstein for all that she has done to promote my work.

Dulce Lamarca, talented photographer.

Barbara HerMor, wonderful assistant and great partner

Arièle Bonzon for this beautiful photo of Mancey, this pretty little village in Burgundy.

Gérard Morin for agreeing to share the story of Bistrot Mancillon.

Principal Letta Belle, who is an unconditional supporter of the Hummingbird Project with her establishment at La Cima Charter School in Brooklyn.

Estelle Julien teacher for the beautiful exchanges between the students of La Cima in Brooklyn and those of her class in Damparis.

Mia Reynolds-Bird, who is now a 5th grade student, for her beautiful text in her Secret Bag and her daily presence during the "zooms meeting" from March to June 2020.

Dr. Tracie C. Thiam for 18 years of trust and care.

Agnes Violet my sister, for the wonderful gift of her "Madame Chiffon" who traveled in a few days during the pandemic between Dakar and New York to be in my book.

Sophie Schrago for her translation from French to English.

Layla Malek Tabbal and the CALEC team for putting the book together.

Notes

Mara and Dann. Doris Lessing.

(1) Oliver Mtukudzi: Zimbabwean musician, businessman, philanthropist, human rights activist and UNICEF Goodwill Ambassador for the Southern Africa region. Tuku was considered Zimbabwe's cultural icon. He died aged 66 in January 2019.

(2) Tamatave is also called Toamasina in Malagasy. It is a port located on the east coast of Madagascar. It is a tourist town and a provincial capital.

(3) leaves of Ravenala, better known in French as the traveller's tree. Emblem of Madagascar, it is a herbaceous plant and not a tree. The ravenala has many properties and is used for many things. In addition to being a medicinal plant, its most spectacular use is in the island of Sainte-Marie where entire villages are made from the different parts of this plant: dried leaves (or falafa) as a covering for the roof, the stems for the walls and the trunk for the floor. Everything is used.

(4) Bed: small growing space the size of a single bed in New York City Community Gardens.

(5) NYCHA: The New York City Housing Authority, or NYCHA, is a public agency of the New York government that administers public housing and low-income housing in New York City's five boroughs. The organization was established in 1934.

(6) The famous Vonette: Vonette was a local glory, a very chrismatic woman known for her very strong character

(7) Bistrot Mancillon: for information, the term "Mancillon" designates the native inhabitants of Mancey while the term

"Manceans" designates all the inhabitants of the village.

(8) The Bronx: The Bronx is one of the five boroughs of New York City.

(9) George Floyd. May 29, 2021: The death of African American G. Floyd suffocated under the knee of a white police officer in Minneapolis (in the State of Minnesota) sparked national and global outrage, carried by the Black lives Matters movement worldwide.

Post Scriptum

Gary Samuels, I wrote these pages listening to the gospels you sang so well. You see, you didn't leave us at the start of the pandemic in the spring of 2020, music doesn't die.

About TBR Books

TBR Books is a program of the Center for the Advancement of Languages, Education, and Communities. We publish researchers and practitioners who seek to engage diverse communities on topics related to education, languages, cultural history, and social initiatives. We translate our books in a variety of languages to further expand our impact.

📖 BOOKS IN ENGLISH

The Heart of an Artichoke by Linda Ashour and Claire Lerognon

French All Around us by Kathleen Stein-Smith and Fabrice Jaumont

Navigating Dual Immersion: A Teacher's Companion for the School Year and Beyond by Valerie Sun

Conversations on Bilingualism by Fabrice Jaumont

One Good Question: How to Ask Challenging Questions that Lead You to Real Solutions by Rhonda Broussard

Bilingual Children: Families, Education, and Development by Ellen Bialystok

Can We Agree to Disagree? by Sabine Landolt and Agathe Laurent

Salsa Dancing in Gym Shoes by Tammy Oberg de la Garza and Alyson Leah Lavigne

Beyond Gibraltar; The Other Shore; Mamma in her Village by Maristella de Panizza Lorch

The Clarks of Willsborough Point by Darcey Hale

The English Patchwork by Pedro Tozzi and Giovanna de Lima

Peshtigo 1871 by Charles Mercier

The Word of the Month by Ben Lévy, Jim Sheppard, Andrew Arnon

Two Centuries of French Education in New York: The Role of Schools in Cultural Diplomacy by Jane Flatau Ross

The Bilingual Revolution: The Future of Education is in Two Languages by Fabrice Jaumont

📖 BOOKS IN OTHER LANGUAGES

Deux siècles d'enseignement français à New York : le rôle des écoles dans la diplomatie culturelle by Jane Flatau Ross

Sénégalais de l'étranger by Maya Smith

Le projet Colibri : créer à partir de "rien" by Vickie Frémont

Pareils mais différents by Sabine Landolt and Agathe Laurent

Le don des langues by Kathleen Stein-Smith and Fabrice Jaumont

📖 BOOKS FOR CHILDREN (available in several languages)

Franglais Soup e by Adrienne Mei

Rainbows, Masks, and Ice Cream by Deana Sobel Lederman

Korean Super New Years with Grandma by Mary Chi-Whi Kim and Eunjoo Feaster

Math for All by Mark Hansen

Rose Alone by Sheila Decosse

Uncle Steve's Country Home; The Blue Dress; The Good, the Ugly, and the Great by Teboho Moja

Immunity Fun!; Respiratory Fun!; Digestive Fun! By Dounia Stewart-McMeel

Marimba by Christine Hélot, Patricia Velasco, Antun Kojton

Our books are available on our website and on all major online bookstores as paperback and e-book. Some of our books have been translated in over a dozen languages. For a listing of all books published by TBR Books, information on our series, or for our submission guidelines for authors, visit our website at:

www.tbr-books.org

About CALEC

The Center for the Advancement of Languages, Education, and Communities (CALEC) is a nonprofit organization focused on promoting multilingualism, empowering multilingual families, and fostering cross-cultural understanding. The Center's mission is in alignment with the United Nations' Sustainable Development Goals. Our mission is to establish language as a critical life skill, by developing and implementing bilingual education programs, promoting diversity, reducing inequality, and helping to provide quality education. Our programs seek to protect world cultural heritage and support teachers, authors, and families by providing the knowledge and resources to create vibrant multilingual communities.

The specific objectives and purpose of our organization are:

- To develop and implement education programs that promote multilingualism and cross-cultural understanding, and establish an inclusive and equitable quality education, including internship and leadership training. [SDG # 4, Quality Education]

- To publish and distribute resources, including research papers, books, and case studies that seek to empower and promote the social, economic, and political inclusion of all, with a focus on language education and cultural diversity, equity, and inclusion. [SDG # 10, Reduced Inequalities]

- To help build sustainable cities and communities and support teachers, authors, researchers, and families in the advancement of multilingualism and cross-cultural understanding through collaborative tools for linguistic communities. [SDG # 11, Sustainable Cities and Communities]

- To foster strong global partnerships and cooperation, and mobilize resources across borders, to participate in events and activities that promote language education through knowledge sharing and coaching, empowering parents, and teachers, and building multilingual societies. [SDG # 17, Partnerships for the Goals]

SOME GOOD REASONS TO SUPPORT US

Your donation helps:

- develop our publishing and translation activities so that more languages are represented.
- provide access to our online book platform to daycare centers, schools, and cultural centers in underserved areas.
- support local and sustainable action in favor of education and multilingualism.
- implement projects that advance dual-language education
- organize workshops for parents, conferences with large audiences, meet-the-author chats, and talks with experts in multilingualism.

DONATE ONLINE

For all your questions, contact our team by email at contact@calec.org or donate online on our website:

www.calec.org

www.ingramcontent.com/pod-product-compliance
Lightning Source LLC
Chambersburg PA
CBHW040304170426
43194CB00021B/2895